AF326866

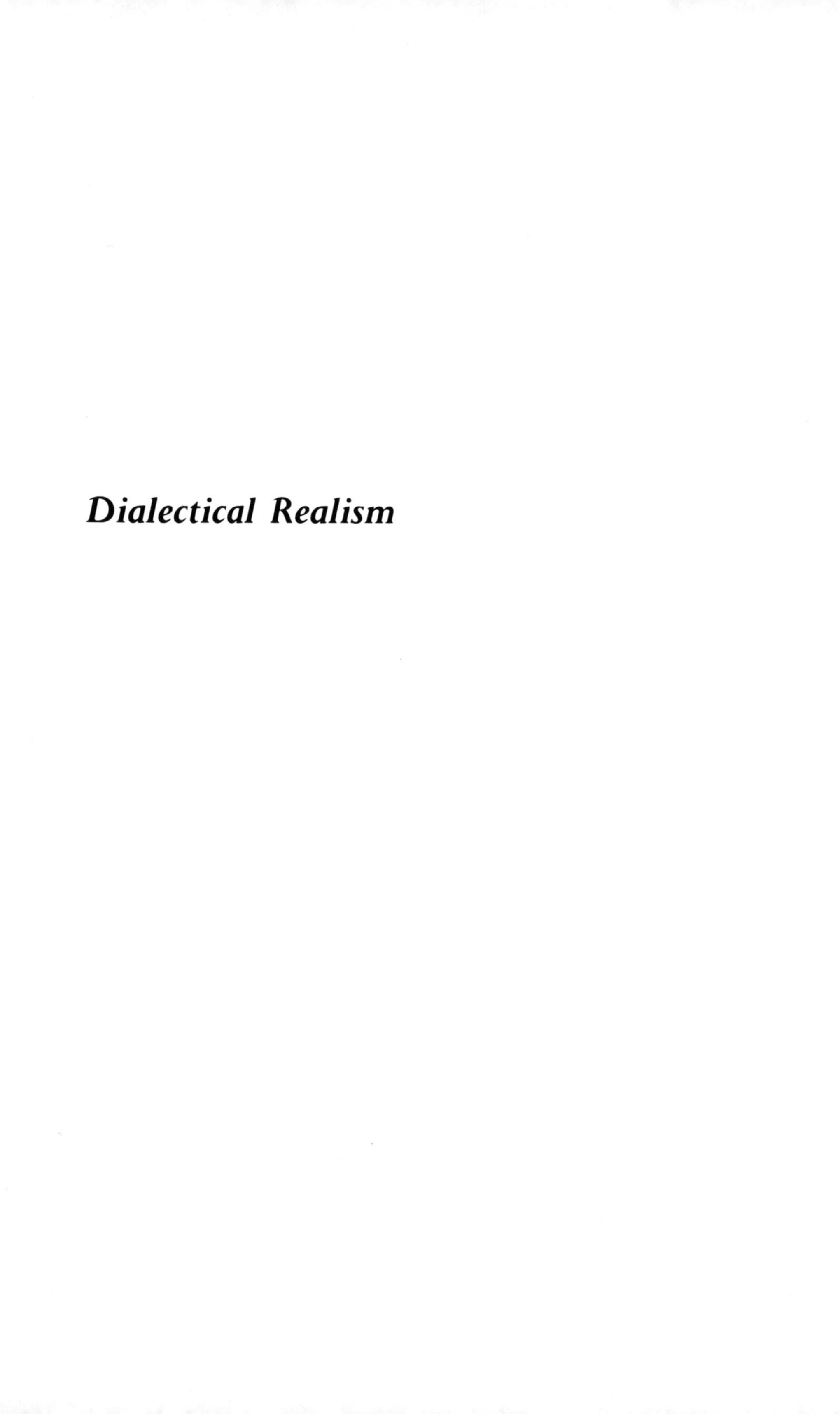

Dialectical Realism

Dialectical Realism

Towards a Philosophy of Growth

Yves Chesni, M.D.

Specialist in nervous and mental diseases
Former director
of the *Service Médico-Pédagogique*, Geneva, Switzerland
Vice-president
of the International Stress and Tension Control Society

Translated from the French by
Joseph P. Zenk, Ph.D.

The Live Oak Press, Palo Alto

Library of Congress Cataloging-in-Publication Data

Chesni, Yves.
Dialectical realism.

Translation of: Réalisme dialectique.
Bibliography: p.
1. Knowledge, Theory of. 2. Relation (Philosophy) 3. Growth. I.
Title. [DNLM: 1. Ego. 2. Human Development. 3. Learning. 4. Philosophy. BD 331 C524r]
BD162.C45 1987   110   86-27726
ISBN 0-931095-00-X

Copyright © 1987, Yves Chesni. All rights reserved including the right of reproduction in any form.

Published by The Live Oak Press, Postal Box 60036, Palo Alto, California U.S.A. 94306.
Manufactured in the United States of America

Also by Yves Chesni:

The Neurological Examination of the Infant, in cooperation with André-Thomas and S. Saint-Anne Dargassies, translated and edited by R. C. MacKleith, P. E. Polani and E. Clayton-Jones. The Spastic Society and Heinemann, London, 1960, reprinted 1964.

Travaux du Service Médico-Pédagogique de Genève, in cooperation with F. Naville, M. Fert, C. Balavoine, A. Menthonnex, R. Guyot, S. Dupuis, E. Amblet, A. Paunier, F. Guignard, F. Martin, A. Grillet. Reprinted from *Médecine et Hygiène,* Médecine et Hygiène, Geneva, 1957.

Réalisme dialectique. Introduction à une philosophie de la croissance. La Baconnière, Neuchâtel, 1973. (Library of Congress card number 74-159365.) Translated here.

Recherches sur le développement de la conscience. La Baconnière, Neuchâtel, 1983. (ISBN 2-8252-0208-8, Library of Congress card number 85-101900.) Translation in progress.

To the memory of
Doctors André-Thomas and Raymond de Saussure, M.D.

To my wife.

Contents

Preface to the American Edition,   viii

Preface,   x

PART ONE—Theory of Knowledge,   1

PART TWO—Theory of Relations,   15

PART THREE—Theory of Development,   29

A. Knowledge of Development and Development of Knowledge,   31

Chapter 1. Knowledge as conscious modification of a subject in relation,   33

Chapter 2. Knowledge of change and of the absence of change,   41

Chapter 3. Determination, indetermination, prevision, creation of the future,   50

Chapter 4. Special modalities of thought, and particularly of the knowledge of time and mistakes about time. Solitude and relation,   56

B. Biological and Human Development,   65

Chapter 1. Mathematical, physico-chemical, and biological points of view regarding the development of living beings,   67

Chapter 2. Relations, drives, emotions, logic, consciousness,   73

Chapter 3. Natural history and philosophies of happiness,   83

Chapter 4. Innate behaviors, maturation, training, and learning,   90

Chapter 5. The liberty of universality and some other senses of the word liberty,   94

Chapter 6. Individual, group, species,   107

Chapter 7. Disillusionment, the awakening of consciousness, and choice,   120

PART FOUR—Economic and Cultural Problems,   129

Chapter 1. Quantitative and qualitative level of employment in its relations with automation, production, consumption, expansion and demography, in different economic systems. General technological relation,   132

Chapter 2. Economic and noneconomic motivations,   142

Chapter 3. The individual worker's debt to the individual, the collectivity, or the group,   147

PART FIVE—Appendices,   151

Letter to Monsieur P.,   153

Some Perspectives on the Dialectical Nature of Progress,   157

Theories of Evolution. Some Doubts and Some Suggestions,   160

Bibliography and Notes,   163

Preface to the American Edition

The main theme of this work is the evaluation of certain basic elements of human sciences according to one fundamental characteristic of human progress, the search for freedom. What is real freedom? What are its conditions? Is it restricted to the recognition and inevitable acceptance of the profound laws of reality? Does freedom imply the power to refuse them? What is meant by responsibility? Sanction? How are freedom and happiness linked?

The first part of the work is devoted to the theory of knowledge. The author is fundamentally a realist and defines his position in opposition to Cartesian idealism, Kantian idealism and their offshoot, Husserl's phenomenology.

The second part is concerned with the theory of knowledge as a particular case of the theory of relationships. A living organism is an original entity in relationship to its surroundings. It is created at least by the interaction of its chromosomes and external factors. During the evolution of species and the progress of civilisation, innate behavior and capacity to learn both contribute to that mobility, memory and coherence which are the conditions for understanding the whole, i.e., for "liberty of universality," or at any rate of the first steps in that direction. In the first two parts, the writer has laid particular stress on originality and relationship. Like all reality, his realism is already dialectic.

The third part is devoted particularly to development. Human advance is not exclusively economic. It consists in an increase of consciousness, in a more adequate comprehension of concrete reality by all our abilities to know, act and love. It is in direct relationship to our "liberty of universality." However the writer also notes the value of catharsis, whether defined in Cartesian, spiritual or psychoanalytical terms or simply by the recognition that a certain progress requires a certain shedding of the inessential. Understanding the whole and the capacity to relate elements to each other and to the whole implies that one is neither blinded, imprisoned, nor submerged by one detail or a mass of them. In the face of neurotic limitations to the "liberty of universality" and the treatment of these unconscious, involuntary and confining automatisms, pathology helps to reveal the normal process and assists in defining the requirements of a freer and happier existence.

The fourth part examines the relationship between human development and economic growth in the light of the general technological relationship which links automation, production, consumption, expansion and the quantitative level of employment. The quality aspect is also studied. The economic and noneconomic motives and the internal requirements of different systems are examined as well as the unquestionable, foreseeable, probable or simply plausible consequences for the development or restriction of humanity in man.

Two short complementary articles summarize and specify the relationship between analytical-synthetic dialectic and conflictual dialectic and the charms as well as the difficulties of Darwin's theory.

The author has provided a selected bibliography with references to personal or group research work. The book is intended not only for his fellow psychiatrists and psychoanalysts and other specialists of human sciences, but also more generally for those possessed of what were once considered the essential attributes of a gentleman: a fair standard of education and a love of true humanity.

Y. Chesni.

Preface

This book treats of what the old humanists used to call the microcosm: man, minuscule in so many ways, limited by what he is, limitless in what he is yet to be, immense in terms of his desire to encompass the world, and sometimes presumptuous to the point of pretending to close off, interdict, limit or fix the boundary of the quest.

The practice of psychophysiology and psychoanalysis, life experiences, encounters, struggles, mutual support, reflection, reading . . . these have provided me with the beginnings of philosophical insight. Philosophy, it is said, can only be based upon experience. Science affords us the most certain experience. Science in its most elevated and profound state is that by which man, the apex of evolution and revolutions, lays hold of himself from within, without forgetting his bodily side nor his relations with what is other than himself. This quality of human sciences sets value not so much on who practices them as on the level of the real which they explore. This in no way gainsays the proper value nor the philosophical impact of other sciences: the two are complementary methods of approaching reality.

The first part of this text was written in October 1968 and presented to some friends; it can serve as a preface. The theory of relations, set forth in the second part, was the object of a lecture at the thirteenth congress of the *Société Française de Médecine de la Voix et de la Parole*. The third part treats of the theory and practice of development and consitutes the body of the work. The fourth part is closely connected with the rest: it would be ridiculous to pretend to deal with human development without understanding its economic base; its text was submitted to various persons and organizations. Each part can be read separately. Throughout the course of this progressive redaction I took into account the observations that people made, and with the help of further information, reflection, and explicitation, I continued along the path of my own development.

May I here express my thanks to all those who have helped me bring this work to completion.

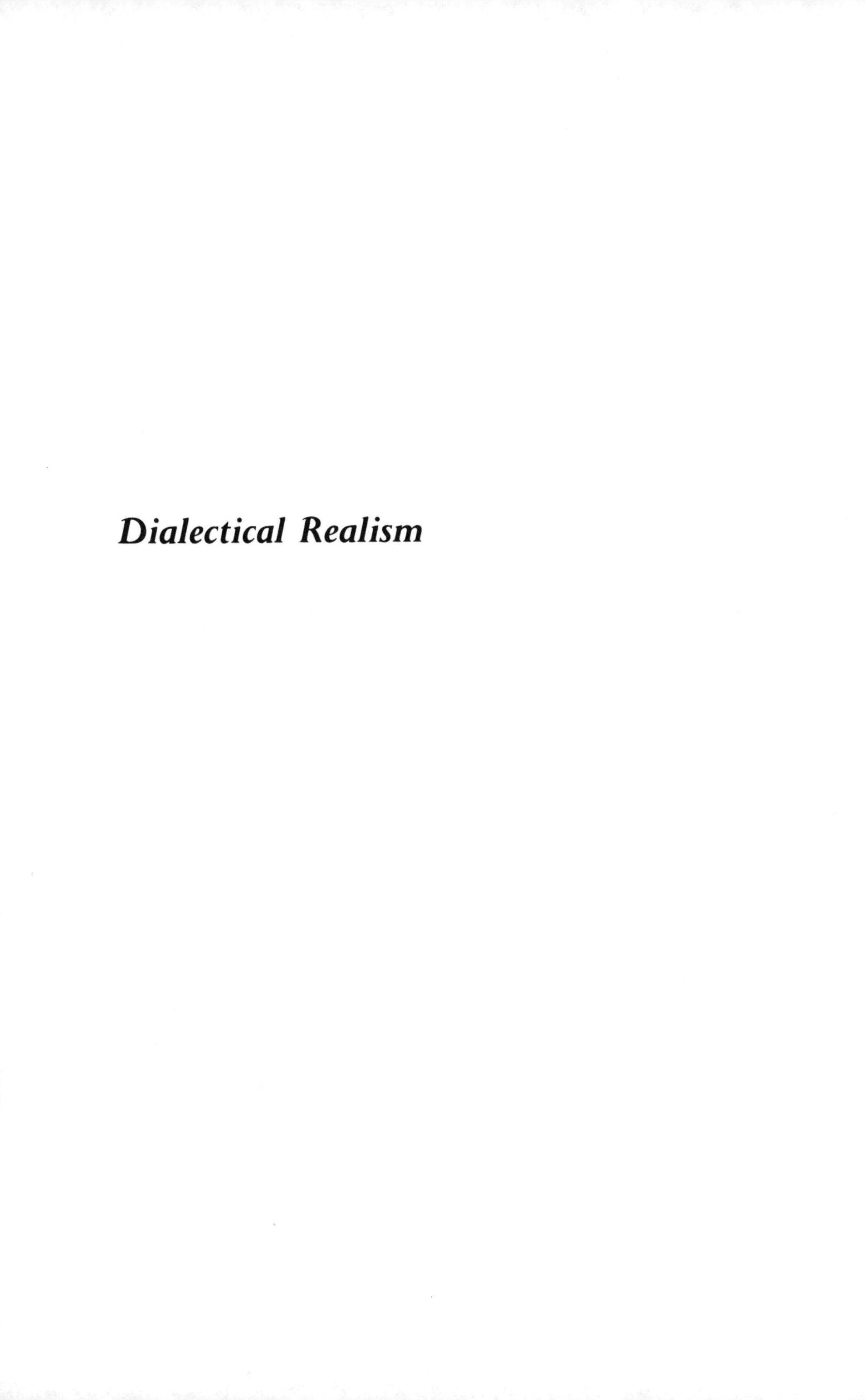

Dialectical Realism

Part One
Theory of Knowledge

Quod vitae sectabor iter?

Dream of Descartes

Man knows himself as having two aspects, an inner and an outer, as an originality with relationships, as permanent and changing. Within himself he feels great powers and desires their blossoming forth.

Consciousness and reason, the authors of freedom, germinate within both animal and young child. In the adult human being, they come to a point at which a qualitative discontinuity takes place. Processes which bear aspects of consciousness and rationality evolve in a way that is partly other than those processes which do not bear them. The fact that the latter precede the former in time, that is anteriority, has nothing to do with superiority. But there is more. "To make," "to have," and "to know" are certainly inter-related, but what is of chief interest to us is the consciousness that we have of the world, of our peers, and of ourselves. If, by some extraordinary event, that consciousness should lessen, and if we should remain capable of transforming the world, what good would that do us?

Granted certain economic factors, and in the absence of other obstacles, man's forces are activated and he tends towards universality. Such is the deep meaning of Engel's letter to Bloch heralding future openings.[1] This tendency is manifested in the struggle for providing all men with the elementary conditions of human development.

These are some initial thoughts about consciousness as relation and as aspect, about permanence and change, unity and multiplicity, and dialectical realism, the theoretical and practical science of our free development, a science which is itself developing freely, a common domain and an open system.

Cartesian exaggerations. Evidence from reality.

Errare humanum est. Without doubt Descartes committed many errors. He looked down upon the senses; he claimed to reduce intellectual knowledge to mathematics; he wanted to demonstrate the existence of things and the value of reason, namely reason's accord with what is other than reason; and he grounded that demonstration in an experience that was certainly deeply human, but whose interpretation is equivocal.

A perfectionist, a doubter and a questionner from infancy, Descartes habitually struggled against the temptations of the senses and the imagination. Over and against them he held up reason and, perhaps partly in compensation and as a defense, surrendered himself to the joys of certitudes of a mathematical nature. He believed he had perceived in a dream his call to know everything and the key to universal knowledge, and elucidated them subsequently in a mathematical physics. He allowed contrary opinions to destroy each other. He loved isolation and used to work while lying in bed. Thus Descartes came to doubt everything, or almost everything. Opinions vary. The senses are often deceptive, as well as the imagination which is derived from them. Dreams are always deceptive. What proof is there that I am not dreaming at this moment?[2]

The steps of Descartes' proof are well known. In order to dream, in order to be deceived, one must at least exist. Pursuing this first clear idea, Descartes successively uncovers three others within it. The idea that God exists in him. God is just and therefore does not deceive. Thus by the same stroke a natural theology, the validity of our belief in the existence of things, and our ability to understand and change them, are all discovered to be grounded in reason by the *cogito*.

Contrary to what Kant was to do, Descartes doubted the existence of things but not the value of his first philosophical intuitions, whether "immediate" or deduced. The notion of the "self" was not discussed. In short, it must be said that his great interior experience demands intepretation within the framework of a *"Weltanschauung,"* of a general concept of the world and ourselves that such an experience seems unable to establish. Indeed, the awareness of a kind of infinity within us was able to be interpreted as an image in man of a creating God, transcendent, indwelling, aspiring,[3] from the naturalistic perspective it became God becoming,[4][5][6] from that of Hegel, God rediscovering himself[7] and in Plato it was interpreted as the soul recalling eternal Ideas . . .

As realists we find no need to demonstrate the existence of a reality independent of the knowledge we have of it. After a certain level of development, that existence enjoys the same immediate evidence as our own thought. Knowing begins with sensation. Even in its most advanced modalities, it is not reducible to mathematics. We take as fact the agreement between reason and that which is other than reason. We tend to explain that agreement by the fact that reason is an aspect of man, that man is a part of the whole, and that the deep laws of reality are the same for each reality.

While claiming to have forsaken it forever, Descartes himself soon rejoined the common view, initially under the title of his provisional morality, and later comforted by his "demonstration." [8] Aside from these few shadows, the light he shed on his times is beyond question.

Knowing as relationship. Psycho-physics. Kant and "phenomenology."
To know is not to coincide, nor is it to be apart, but to be in relationship. Kant appears to have been deceived when he declared that we do not know things but our knowledge of things.[9] The old formula, *"things are within us in a way which is ours,"* even though faulty, at least had the advantage of recalling that in the final analysis knowledge does not know itself while knowing things other than itself. This is also apparently the sense, expressed in the idiom and notions of his times, of Lenin's criticism of certain aberrant elements of Kantianism.[10]

The first term of the knowledge relationship is the whole of what is real, independently of the way it will be known. The second term is the subject able to know. The mental change is a function of these two terms, not of itself. It does not consist of extension in space, but this does not mean that it is unable to be quantified. The objects of psycho-physics are the events common to both physical stimulation[11] and mental change. These common elements could be temporal intervals, identities, differences, etc., at the respective levels of the stimulus and the mental change, abstracted from the concrete manner of being proper to each of the two terms. In the second and third cases, the relationship can be defined as a function of the binary type analogous to that used in electronic calculation.[12] Fechner's psycho-physics ceases to be valid when it pretends to quantify our mental aspect in some other way.[13] The study of thresholds remains such, but the law of logarithms gradually loses interest. This is shown by the transformation now exerted upon a curve originally expressed in decibels to reduce it to a straight, horizontal line, in the measurement of sounds related to hearing, i.e., in an *"audiogram."*

Different, successive qualities and moments are distinguishable in knowing. For instance, after stimulation, at time t_1, t_2, t_3, etc., there arises sensation, then recognition without denomination *(gnosia),* then the word . . . But when B is a function of A, C of B, and D of C, D is a function of A. The process is a series of steps ultimately connected with a reality independent of it. There are no opaque screens between things and us, as Kant and the phenomenologists believed. That does not mean that D is A, nor even, *sensu stricto,* the image of A.

To know means to enter into a relation. We observe that we are able to understand the real and to set it in motion. We tend to explain that ability by the fact that we belong to the whole of what is real and that we ourselves are subject to the deep laws of reality. We grasp elements common to both terms of the relation. In so doing we refer to the dialectical notions of conservation and unity. Should known reality belong to a level of evolution lower than us, there nevertheless exists a certain proportion between it and us. If it exists on the same level as we, the proportion increases: this is what the Ancients were trying to signify when they said that *"like knows like under a mode that is at once its own and that of the like."*

To know is not to coincide. At the heart of relations in the whole of the real, the differences between the terms in rapport characterize our proper originality. That draws us to the dialectical notions of becoming and multiplicity. Even if we know that which is like us, or ourselves, there persists at least a difference of one degree of reflection.

In brief, knowing confronts reality as it is in itself, but for all that we do not confuse ourselves with that which we know. There are identities and differences between the two terms of the relation.

Analysis and synthesis. The notion of aspect.

The process of knowing can be subdivided into several stages: sensation, gnosia, visual image, word, judgment, *"association of ideas,"* and other mental operations. These stages differ among themselves qualitatively and by the interval of time separating their beginnings from the stimulation. In them are distinguishable synthetic and analytic modalities. Analysis and synthesis are intermingled. Each moment exhibits more or less analysis, more or less synthesis: sensory analysis, the synthetic character of judgment, etc. But this does not mean that the other aspect, either analysis or synthesis, is absent at any moment.

A few tenths of a second after the start of adequate stimulation the subject experiences a sensation. It is difficult to distinguish the latter qualitatively from the gnosia that follows, and which contains more predication, more synthesis; the study of the moments at which these interior states arise serves to characterise them. A few tenths of a second after the sensation, the gnosia or nonverbal recognition occurs. And then comes the denomination. These steps are at once analytic and synthetic. They already contain some judgment of existence and some predication, albeit implicit or condensed in the word. The boundary between judgment properly so called and the preceding steps is as hard to establish as that between sensation and recognition. To return to the word, it arises a few tenths of a second after the gnosia and about a half second after the start of stimulation. It is related to the stimulation. Thus when the stimulation is repeated there can be a corresponding repetition of the word, and different words can correspond to sufficient differences. One and the same modification can correspond to a single common area belonging to different concrete individual realities. Such a common area can correspond to an *"essential"* definition, or at least one that is significant according to this or that criterion.[14]

With the intelligible aspects of reality we touch upon some ancient and honored doctrines: that of the one and the many, that of the Ideas, of Being, of being and essence . . . Is the intelligibility of things located in things, in ourselves, or in a transcendent God (or slightly outside such a God, according to the Platonists, out of respect for his unity)?   Let us limit ourselves to the first two of these questions.

Sensible or intelligible, an aspect has no separate existence. It is linked to the reality known and the knowing subject. It characterises their relation. It is analytic and synthetic. To the extent that synthesis has no place, when the datum of analysis is not referred to a real unity, one cannot speak of aspect. Sense aspect is recognized as such in a second moment, at a more elevated degree of knowledge.

Regardless of whether or not it can be reduced to a single word, the definition marks off a part within what Hegel called the organic unity of the whole.[15] Bergson's insistence on this point is well known.[16] It would have been in the interests of the ancient philosophers to have reexamined some of their notions in the perspectives of change and relations in the whole of reality. But, on the other hand, the most authentic dialectic attenuates the accusation that definitions are arbitrary or simply convenient: despite the continuity of series and transitions, evolution seems to proceed in stages when looked upon in the context of change; when considered in a given moment of interrelations, continuity and discontinuity are opposed to each other; finally, we shall see that elements of permanence can be discerned within change. Abstracting, analyzing, delimiting superficially or in depth, in permanence or change, duration or instant, the definition enters the arena of knowledge-as-relation. Not only does reality yield itself to delimitations, it may also have structures within itself, like cleavage planes of a crystal, independent of us; the respective parts of the latter and of our own specific structures, technology, individual histories and utility requirements ought to be considered in each case.

Likewise, within judgment an analytic datum is related synthetically to a certain real unity, and that unification constitutes a new abstracted sameness of the two terms of the knowledge relation: a real unity, independent of us; an attribution of predicate to subject, that is, a synthesis of aspects in a mode proper to our mind. But the unity in consciousness is a function of the unity in the thing, and if the latter is itself set off within the whole of reality, it is not so in a way that is necessarily arbitrary. Intelligence, said the ancients, divides and combines, and in that activity it may or may not ground itself on reality.[17]

The principle of identity, every being is what it is (itself a judgment), would be at the heart of every judgment. As in all judgments we see a synthetic time that links a predicate to a subject. But here predicate and subject bear very visible testimony to a particular modality of knowing: at the same time we abstract being from beings, we declare that there is no being outside of beings, and that the latter are diverse. There would be no contradiction in this analogical abstraction of being, a kind of *"liquid crystal"* serving as the proper domain of our metaphysical intelligence.[18] Be that as it may, the diversification is related to all the partitions of which we have spoken; the least important among them is not that which is within time and change . . .

Association on the basis of common domains itself contains analysis and synthesis. Analogical thought, classification, symbolism, these are but a part of such association. Its importance is such that some have felt that it ought to be the object of a particular philosophy, called *"structuralism."*[19] Everything we have said of knowledge as relation applies to the common domains. Their abstraction and their attribution, both unifying and diversifying, touch upon reality. In each case we must appreciate what are the real planes of separation, the real possibilities of overlapping or insertion, and what comes from our own contribution, ours as endowed with certain structures common to all members of our species, with certain technics, and with an individual history. The contribution of the individual subject can be seen during waking hours and in dreams, in the most flexible and expansive association of ideas as well as in the most automatic and repetitive recollection, either normal or pathological. It can invade the relation to the point of making it disappear, as in certain projective tests; but then another relation arises, that between the subject and itself. Thus the exterior stimulus, whether it has many possible interpretations or is indifferent, as the ink of

Rorschach, is but an occasion to know oneself.

Analytic and synthetic dialectic.

In sum, we know reality under different aspects: sensible or sensorial, intelligible or intellectual, technical, methodological, and even theoretical or dogmatic . . . First of all, this shows that we are in different kinds of relations with it. It also shows that these relations have a double modality, analytic and synthetic. Synthesis, itself a function of the unity of the "thing," draws the data of analysis into the unity of the "object" and so prevents us from turning them separately into complete realities through what might be called a mistaken reification. In a way the problem is taken to a higher level when we take into account the demarcation of "realities" within the whole of reality. The composition of the two kinds of criteria, that is of the various levels of knowledge and of its analytic or synthetic modalities, completes the sense-intelligence dialectic already envisaged by Plato.[20]

It has recently become fashionable to distinguish between the dialectic of nature and the dialectic of thought. That, surprisingly enough, within a certain framework that seems to make of thought an epiphenomenon of the body.[21] We feel it is more judicious to subdivide dialectic into dialectic of the real in general and dialectic of man in particular. In the latter, before envisaging the notion of both contradictory thesis and antithesis yielding to a synthesis, we would do well to consider what might be called a dialectic of aspects. Anticipating somewhat the following chapters, we are from now on in a position to discern a fundamental modality in human progress: the ever increasing multiplication and precision of aspects under which we know the world and ourselves; the correct evaluation of the notion of aspect; the sudden or progressive recognition of aspects as such with their double characteristic of analysis and synthesis; the overcoming of an illusory reification of the data of analysis and an inadequate hierarchization of them, which is a frequent consequence of such reification.

The technics pass through ceaseless higher planes of perfection and diversification. They prolong and amplify our senses and our intellectual capacity, not only in the sense of exterior instruments but equally as well in the sense of conceptual models, theoretical and practical points of view, working hypotheses, etc. . . . However poorly developed in comparison with sciences devoted to understanding, transforming, and dominating the exterior world, in greatest part catering to our material needs as consumers and our love of power, the sciences which consider man have nevertheless made some little progress. Stimulated by the practical needs of medicine we discovered our physiological and neurological aspects. The physiology of behavior, enlightened by Jackson's evolutionism, benefitted from Pavlov's marvelous discoveries about typology and conditioning. Psychoanalysis, sociology, the theory and practice of the "struggle for life" and of mutual assistance, have joined classic introspective psychology. An evolutionist and revolutionary point of view has supplanted a fixist one. Replacing man at the heart of relations within the totality and particularly in his social context, ontogeny, i.e., the science of individual development, began to reveal to us the instinctual, affective, and intellectual aspects of human growth, the way in which habits are formed, the conditions of a structured, coherent actualization of our powers and of accession to true liberty.

Corporeal and mental aspects. Psychophysiology. Reductionisms and dualisms.

After the moment t_0 of interaction between the subject and an external stimulus at moments t_1, t_2, t_3, t_4 . . . occur those introspective modifications which we call sensation, gnosia or nonverbal recognition, word, image, judgment, etc. . . . . From the physiological point of view, the intervals of time between t_0 and the other different moments correspond to the propagation of nerve impulses along structures more and more distant from the peripheral sense organ, and of increasing complexity, that involves an increasing number of neurones and synapses. Pathology highlights certain differences. For example in the so called "amnesic aphasia", the gnosia or nonverbal recognition takes place normally, but if the denomination occurs it does so after a considerable delay. Repeating the stimulus accelerates the denomination, an acceleration which happens in other processes as well, whether normal or pathological. From the physiological point of view this is probably explainable in terms of synaptic facilitation.[22]

Our anatomical and physiological aspect and our conscious one are *sui generis* and also in a way heterogeneous, if only because the one deals with the extended and is subject to certain kinds of measurement while the other is not. Nevertheless, from both of them can be abstracted a certain number of common elements, as we have just shown. These common elements connote the unity of the subject. They constitute the proper object of psychophysiology, at least in a very limited and precise modality. Despite the obscurities which still exist, from now on we have at our disposal sufficient proofs that all our conscious modifications, from the most elementary to the most elaborate, from the most passive to the most active, from sensation to intelligence, are introspective aspects of a reality that is unitary though partially changing: ourselves, who exhibit corresponding physiological aspects. Henceforth we are able to carry on completely both analysis and synthesis so to say throughout the knowing subject taken as the object of knowledge. This does not mean that every defined psychological modification has a unique anatomophysiological correspondent. Think, for example, of the phenomenon of substitution . . .[23]

There is no doubt that a certain part of ancient philosophy, which attempted reasonably to ground itself on what we call experience, was built on insufficient experience. Ignorance of our own neurophysiological aspects had disastrous consequences for the theory of knowledge. Indeed, what should we today think of affirmations such as the following: *the body is not required for intellectual activity after the fashion of an organ, but because of the object it provides, that is, the phantasm.*[24] The attentive reading of other texts of the period is no less instructive. The sense organs are known. They are looked upon somewhat like the anatomophysiological, corporeal aspect of a process whose introspective aspects are sensation and the phantasm. On the other hand the neurophysiological aspects of subsequent modifications of the subject are unknown, modifications whose conscious aspects are nonverbal recognition, verbalization, judgment, etc. . . . As a result they are omitted, and intelligence is separated and reified. Not completely, however, for it is observed that it follows sensation and imagination, whose corporeal concomitants are known. Intelligence needs the body, therefore, to furnish the sensation and the image, and for that alone; in this way is explained the fact that thinking can cause fatigue even though it has no corporeal concomitants of its own. Synthesis reached as far as sensation and phantasm because analysis extended to their corporeal aspects. It had no place after the phantasm because analysis had not yet discovered the further neurophysiological aspect. Taken in isolation, the intellectual act remains connected to what precedes it, but like a bubble trapped by sensation and the phantasm, and with them by the body. The last mentioned is close to being denigrated. We are a long way from the prudence of St. Paul, who told of once being taken up to the third heaven but had the care to add that he knew not whether it was with the body or without it.[25] [26]

Ignorance of our highest neural activity has contributed to all sorts of shoddy thinking about such matters as the concrete and the abstract, the sensible and the intelligible, corporeal and noncorporeal, material and nonmaterial, act and potency. The senses and the imagination have a twofold connection with matter: they are in touch with the individual, concrete characteristics of the exterior realities known through them; and they have corporeal organs. Intelligence enjoys a threefold divorce from matter: it abstracts from the individual, concrete characteristics of the known exterior realities; it has no corporeal organ, that is, it lacks neurophysiological concomitants; and it is act, or form.

A few centuries later, Descartes found himself torn between this philosophical position and the earliest progress of neurophysiology. At the same time that he was formulating the psychophysiological hypothesis in almost modern terms, he kept a radical separation between the body and the spirit at every stage from the sensation to the intellectual act. Cartesian dualism held for correspondence between our aspects and at the same time continued to affirm their total heterogeneity. Descartes misconstrued the notion of aspects. He wrongly divided and reified them. He tried in vain to understand the connections between them. He glimpsed the synthesis but never achieved it. An analogous way of thinking is found in part even in the philosophy of Bergson.

Finally, after the thesis, after an unfortunate attempt at synthesis shattered, the antithesis arose. Physiology grew apace. Evolution became known. God grew to be an embarrassment, or at least the popular idea of Him. Now our corporeal aspect was spotlighted, isolated, separated, reified. In Nature, the processes which bear no conscious or rational aspects are first in the order of change, and they are therefore first in the order of value. The brain secretes thought, or, what amounts to the same thing, thought is a cerebral function.[27] It is an epiphenomenon. The current style is to simulate ignorance of it in favor of the physiology of behavior, or even of I.B.M. equipment.

For us, our deepest thoughts and the most modest of our sensations are aspects of ourselves. Here below at least, to each of our introspective aspects whether simply conscious or at once conscious and logical, that is rational, there correspond anatomophysiological aspects. Common elements can be abstracted from these two sorts of aspects. The former underscore the unity of the subject. At the same time we think of knowledge as a relationship between the whole and the part, between reality and the subject capable of knowing it. The two terms of the relationship, the first term and the change of consciouness of the second term resulting from contact with each other, are partly heterogeneous and partly homogeneous. Without going so far as to confuse them, the two also have common elements. These underscore the unity of the whole. When man studies his own knowing, a difference of one degree of reflection persists. We observe the relations existing within the whole of the real and also our own proper originality, both conservation and emergence.

Geneva
October 1968

Part Two
Theory of Relations

Conference at the Thirteenth Congress of the French Society of Voice and Speech Medicine, Paris, October 5, 1971. Revue de Laryngologie, *93*, nos. 3-4, Portmann, Bordeaux, 1972.

Dialectical Realism and the Theory of Knowledge.

In our opinion, reality contains originalities in relationships, and exhibits permanence and change. It is dialectical in several senses. Man is real, dialectical, a part of reality, and he is inclined to enter into relationships with realities that are themselves real, realistic, and dialectical. In these relationships he appears to follow ways that are common and ways that are properly his own.

For Plato, dialectic was the movement of human thought in its incessant oscillation between the sensible and the intelligible, between the world of senses, called illusion, and that of the Ideas, considered full reality.[28] [29] For Aristotle, it was the art of speaking with a semblance of truth, but not with certitude; it had a pejorative air to it. For Hegel dialectic was the movement of the Spirit, initially incarnated (lost rather than born) in things here below, and then growing in self-consciousness in man, in philosophy, and in Hegel. Towards the end of his life Hegel denied having rediscovered ancient Indian pantheism without realizing it.[30] Whether pantheist, semi-pantheist, or something else, Marx and Lenin ascribed Hegel's dialectic to Plato's idealism and purported to set it back on its own feet. No longer is there a descent of the Spirit, of the Concept, into the world. No longer are there reflections, a sphere of shadow, participation in the Ideas or Essences in the mind of God; instead we have ascending evolution and revolutions in which the greater issues from the lesser. God is dead, or in a certain fashion creates himself.[31] [32]

Etymologically, *dia* has a gamut of senses well suited, we shall see, to our purposes: "across time and space; in regard to alteration, the absence of alteration, the moment; with or without the idea of violent penetration, of tearing away, separation, conflict; in an opaque, resistant climate, or an open and free one; with or without obstacle; at a distance in time and space; element, means, cause, superiority, achievement, perfection . . ." *Lego, legomai, lectikos* will serve to make the sense precise and will add mention of the relationship setting, of dialog, gathering together, synthesizing, sorting out, choosing, signifying, saying . . . In dialog there can be opposition, aspects, a surmounting, a synthesizing . . . Reality, from *res,* can be understood in two different and conjoined senses, as when the whole is divided into its parts: *"rem universam tribuere in partes"* (Cicero). It concerns, if you will, the thing-in-itself, the *Gegenstand* of Kant, that reality which is independent of the knowledge and action relationships that we set about to establish with it; but contrary to Kant, we do not declare it to be unknowable. It concerns also originalities in relation. In the latter case it may be well to ask whether they constitute merely a simple puzzle effect involving arbitrary analysis and synthesis, an artificial "thingification" of reality.[33]

Indeed, he who speaks of relation speaks of terms in relation (in the sense, for example, of a mathematical function), and in so doing brings up the problem of how reality is partitioned. So it is first necessary to study the theory of knowledge, but without failing to entertain the question whether or not we may be traveling in a circle. After all we are defining knowledge as a relation between two terms without first examining the notion of terms in relation. On this point we have a feel for the obvious. Contrary to Descartes we think that it is superfluous and probably impossible to demonstrate the existence of the first term. It seems to us, as it did to Kant, that we do not coincide with it, which is another way of saying that we are at least partly different from it; but for us this is not the same as saying that we do not know it. To put it briefly, we feel that the breaking or at least the attenuation of the circle lies in the fact that there are indemonstrable truths. The ancient philosophers had already come to this realization. Among those truths there are the existence of two terms, a certain difference betweeen them, and the establishing of a relationship between them: the knowledge of the other, or, more exactly, of the partially other; or, the knowledge of the self in as much as the self is different from that knowledge. So we have no scruples about basing our exploration of relations initially upon the example of a certain relation called knowledge, and at the same time doing so by means of that relation.

Knowledge as relationship and as aspect. Successive moments.

After its encounter with an efficient physical stimulus at moment t_0, there arise (at moments t_1, t_2, etc.) within the subject several mental modifications: sensation, gnosia or nonverbal recognition, the word spoken aloud or within, or mental speech. Then there are judgment, explicit or implicit, and other mental operations more or less complex and more or less discursive, association of ideas, etc. . . . . The first temporal intervals are of the order of a few tenths of a second; normally the word occurs no sooner than half a second after an object breaks into view. From the anatomophysiological perspective, these temporal intervals correspond to the sum of the times involved in axonal and synaptic conduction from the peripheral sensorial organs to nerve areas more and more distant, more and more rich in neurons, and more and more complex, with feedback in certain cases.[34] Aside from certain initial experiments by Jung, the *tempo* of the emotional changes remains unexplored.

Clearly the mental aspect differs from the physical stimulus and from the anatomophysiological aspect first of all because it is never extended in space (which is not to say that it is unquantifiable). Further, each of the successive conscious modifications differs from the others and possesses its own proper, *sui generis* characteristics. But we feel that between the two terms of the relationship, between each of the successive changes of the subject, and between its respective mental and anatomophysiological aspects there are not only differences; there are also identities and common elements. Among these are identities (repetition), differences, analogies involving both identities and differences, simultaneous occurences and nonsimultaneous ones (succession), the number of successive modifications, their order of succession, and the temporal intervals between them.[35] These common elements are abstracted from more concrete modalities proper, respectively, to each of the two terms, to the successive modifications of the second term (the subject), and to each of its aspects. There could be many precisions, reservations, and exceptions made, and these would no doubt confirm the rule, but this brief exposition must have some limits. Let us simply point out Bergson's critique of the states of consciousness[36] as well as Leibnitz's remark on the confusion between the identical and the indiscernable.[37]

For the second time we need to ask ourselves whether we are proceeding in a circle and are guilty of a tautology. To affirm the existence of these common elements is, from the part of the observer, to know them, and it is knowledge that is precisely in question. In attempting to limit ourselves to the physical stimulus we still see that the observer can know it in a different way than the subject; he can consider it in wider and wider relations involving reagents other than the subject, himself, other witnesses of the same species, his theoretical and practical devices for analysis, measurement, identification, prediction, and fabrication: animals, plants, natural physical and chemical systems, etc . . . . There seems to be a community of reactions, and here, it appears, we have an initial way to forestall the eventual tautology. Practice —*praxis*— is particularly enlightening. If someone like Newton had, perhaps while distracted, warmed up his watch while checking an egg for the time, the consequences arising from the error, brief though it may have been, would quickly serve to shed light on identity and difference. Indeed, as we were pointing out a moment ago, there are some truths it would be well to avoid wanting to demonstrate, such as the fact that a watch is not an egg, that to know one or the other is not the same as to become one or the other, etc. . . . .

To say that there are common elements between the two terms of the knowledge relationship, and particularly between the stimulus and the successive mental modifications of the subject, is to say that at no level of knowledge is there any phenomenal or categorical screen between us and reality. The whole is completely heterogeneous to none of its parts, and no one part is heterogeneous to any of the others.[38]

The existence of common elements both in a longitudinal sense, common to the first term and to the successive modifications of the second, and in a transversal sense, common to the respectively mental and anatomophysiological aspects of the subject at all the degrees of knowledge, has another consequence. It is no longer possible to maintain that only sensation and the phantasm, the latter usually meaning a visual representation or "image," are concomitant with corporeal activity. If we are to hold to the texts, it appears that an entire theory of the intellectual soul has been founded upon ignorance of a part of our anatomophysiological aspects. This simply means that in the time of Aristotle and St. Thomas Aquinas (even thought the former had a school of dissection), the eye was known but not the brain.[39] Galen had a kind of feeling about that omission. In more distant times the longitudinal division was pushed even closer to sensorial origins: Socrates thought that neither the image nor the memory in general, even when senselike or representative, had any corporeal concomitants. There is no doubt that dreams had a hand in this, as well as epileptic seizures of the temporal lobe in the old theory of reminiscence . . .

Analysis and synthesis.

Spirit, says Aristotle, divides and composes, and not necessarily in an arbitrary way. Saint Thomas translated that by *"intellectus componentis et dividentis, habens fundamentum in re."* Since things themselves are rooted in God, the Ideas of Plato were only partially involved here below, but possibly less motionless than the critic usually paints them. The second part of the proposition has to do with unities, with cleavage points within the real, independent of the fact that we know them. This is somewhat reminiscent of our first approach to identity and difference, when without any excess of theoretical scruples we distinguished between the knowing subject and that which the subject knows, between the egg and the watch, and between both and their owner. A third time we have a sense of being in a circle and yet find the difficulty surmountable, if only by the realization that every demonstration is impossible and superfluous except demonstration by the absurd. The notions of real identity, difference and originality do not exclude the fact that these unities of the real are, in some way, intertwinings of relations, points of intersection in the whole, moments of becoming. Nor does it mean that sometimes the separations cannot be completely arbitrary. Analysis and synthesis characterize the relationship between two terms, and the terms upon which they depend vary case by case: sometimes upon one, sometimes upon the other, and sometimes upon both in different proportions. Let us leave it to the mathematicians to put all this into formulas.

In varying proportions and modalities, analysis and synthesis are encountered at every step of the knowing process such as we have described it, at each of its moments and successive modalities. If it is true that sensation itself has a certain grasp of exterior origin that is of an existence distinct from that of the subject (more exactly from that of the sensation), then sensorial analysis is already attended by the ghost of an implicit attribution. There is a putting-into-relation, and in that sense there is synthesis. This increases as the data of various analyzers confront each other. In gnosia, that is nonverbal recognition, identification, and classification, the data of sensorial analysis are related to the unity of a concrete individuality (unity of identity) or of a class allowing identities and differences (unity of analogy). These unities themselves result from a preliminary delimitation more or less based upon reality. The word expresses gnosia, resumes it, and makes it more precise. Formal judgement explicitly attributes the predicate to the subject, etc. . . . In addition to that it seems that very often we relate the data of analysis to each other without reducing them to a concrete individual unity or to a class. There is, if you will, a synthesis in the sense of putting-into-relation, of drawing together, of composition, but here we are dealing with a modality of synthesis that is different from the other two.

Thus different modalities and proportions of analysis and synthesis appear at different moments in the development of a discrete process of knowing for an adult, the whole of which takes place within a relatively brief period of time. The same can be said for all phylogeny, ontogeny, and the history of civilizations. Analytic and synthetic dialectic do not coincide entirely with the dialectic of sense and intelligence, nor with that of contradiction . . . at least not with a certain kind of contradiction. We have seen a noteworthy example of the former in the progressive knowledge of our respectively mental and anatomophysiological, corporeal aspects as those of a subject that is, so to speak, unitary from head to toe. A great part of the progress of thought is made in this way.[40]

Aspect is at once analytic and synthetic. In a sense, the object is even more analytic. It is in no way to be confused with the first term of the relation. The first term is the whole of the reality independent of the relation that we are going to have with it. We might say that the object constitutes a first delimitation of the reality by the subject in the sense of an operational field, or even succesive operational fields. It depends upon the two terms. It characterizes a certain analytic modality of the relationship. It is no more a simple projection, a simple subjective construction, than the patient is for the surgeon, or the stomach lining, and the malignant appendix; if need be this new comparison should serve to reassure us against the eventual tautology. But it does make us wary in the use of such formulas as "objective term," "relation between subject and object," "objective relations," etc. . . . If the notion of potency were more clear, we would be happy to say of the first term that it contains all possible objects, and without pessimism, probably much more.

Just as the object, the effective stimulus, sign, or signal characterizes a first analytic modality of the relationship: indeed its delimitation and efficiency are a function of the subject as well. Let us note in passing that stimulus and object are sometimes given different meanings in the same text: thus the breakdown of homeostasis is called an internal stimulus that arouses internal senses and brings about drives, emotions, behaviors like hunger and thirst, eating and drinking, etc.; but in such a case it is customary to say that the drive achieves an *ad hoc* satisfaction by means of adequate exterior objects. Further the object here has reference to an affective relationship, in other words a relationship that is largely one of drives and emotions.

Reciprocal adaptation, truth, logic, reason.

"To be adapted or not to be." Paraphrasing Hamlet we can doubtless affirm that every living being, and perhaps even every being, is either in some way adapted or it is not. This includes the sense of reciprocal adaptation: the living organism adapts itself to its environment, adapts the environment to itself, and *vice-versa*. In a general way, reciprocal adaptation signifies a certain agreement between the two terms of the relation. To put it in another way, a certain kind of truth. On the side of the subject and even that of the two terms in relation, the behavior which assures this mutual agreement can be qualified as logic. Logic is therefore defined initially by the

relation, and more precisely by the truth of the relation, by the mutual agreement of its two terms.[41] In mathematical reasoning, for example, the subject's behavior can be disassociated from the first term for a certain period of time and in a certain way. What is logical then in a primary sense requires that if the premises are true, that is, in agreement with the whole of the real, then the conclusions are equally true. In a derived sense one can still speak of the logical if the internal mechanisms remain the same as in the above case but the conclusions are incorrect, i.e., not adapted to the whole of reality, because the premises were either false or incomplete. So it is that there are different geometries. We call "reason" conscious logic, and also, it seems, one that intervenes in a relation that is sufficiently universal in a sense that we will be describing. Like logic, reason is ordered toward truth.

If we should see ever so little, what we perceive all about us is a mutual agreement of terms in relation that we may call an outline of truth, and behaviors designed to maintain, increase and diversify that mutual agreement, which is the rough outline of logic and reason. This truth and logic in "inanimate" things, in living beings and in ourselves, admit of common grounds and originalities. Teilhard de Chardin spoke of this as conservation and emergence. Engels spoke in terms of levels of dialectic, reversing Hegel and, as did Hegel, seeing clearly that all that precedes is not destroyed by what follows.[42] The least chemical reaction, the growth of a crystal, the autoreproduction of long genetic molecules and the direction they give for individual growth, these all exhibit identifications, differentiations, structures of order and space, of succession and interlocking. The principles of identity and noncontradiction, in the ontological sense and that of formal logic, reign along with their correlatives, reciprocal adaptation and mutual agreement, in brief, the truth. In our opinion this is one of the great lessons to be derived from such authors as Lwoff,[43] Monod,[44] and Jacob.[45]

In this community of conduct, of the order of logic and truth, of mutual agreement of terms in relationship, Kant would have seen a simple projection of our *a priori* forms of sensibility and our categories of meaning. We, however, see in it the explanation of our ability to understand the real, an ability that implies a certain community of origin and the conservation of certain common domains. For the sake of preciseness or otherwise, we should add to the previously described elements common to the two terms of the knowledge relation what we said in regard to truth and logic modalities within general and common relational behaviors. A moment ago it seemed to us that this community of reaction at the interior of systems more vast than the subject, the observer, even human kind, confirms and even replaces the observer's judgment relative to the first term of the relation under study, at least relative to a part of the first term, such as the sign, the signal, the stimulus or object, and so serves to avoid or reduce a possible tautology. Now we are presenting these common behaviors as an indication of conservation, of nontotal heterogeneity, and at the same stroke as an explanation of the ability to know. Might it not be appropriate to ask for a fifth time whether we are involved in a tautology? With regard to knowing whether reciprocal adaptation may not be a simple puzzle effect or the consequence of arbitrary delimitations, as could the existence of original beings in relations, these matters were discussed when we were speaking of the real bases for analysis and synthesis.

The subordination of logic to relation, more precisely the relation of a truthful, suitable, and reciprocal adaptation, is seemingly no more than a consequence or aspect of the imperative governing all living beings, and even all of beings: to be adapted or not to be, or to cease to exist. This is seen in phylogeny, in ontogeny, in the history of societies. Its observation is the entire work of naturalists, psychologists, and sociologists, to say nothing of the physicians and chemists who should be cited here. With André-Thomas we once made a modest contribution to this field ourselves.[46] We have come back to it many times, in different ways, and from different perspectives. Let us limit ourselves to observe that a simple momentary separation from the external world, as in a dream, is accompanied by a weakness, disorders, breaks in our logical apparatus; causality, identity and noncontradiction will sometimes reach the point of almost disappearing without our experiencing the least surprise. Analogous observations can be made about contents that are repressed, neurotic, unconscious, "nonrelational," or at least have ceased to be in relation. As for dreams, this does not mean that they cannot at times have great logical force and truth value for the present.[47] As for neurotic complexes, they may have at one time corresponded to behaviors that were logical and adapted, but they have become disrelated, illogical and false.

Degrees of independence of the phenotype in relation to a genotype taken as defined in a certain way. Tendency towards universality. Two senses of the word liberty.
Among others, one line of evolution and revolutions is characterised by a quantitative and qualitive enrichment of living organisms with conscious-

ness, reciprocal adaptation, logic, truth, and reason. In this can be discerned a tendency towards universality in the sense of an individual relation that is increasingly complete within wider and wider wholes, of a growing ability to compare the different parts with themselves and with the whole, without, so to speak, allowing one among them to be blinding or imprisoning. It is, if you will, a tendency towards liberty in a first sense of the word. As for knowing if one is free or not to make oneself free or to remain a prisoner of the partial, that, it seems, is a second sense of the word liberty. For now we will not be dealing with the latter. Like many other considerations presented here, its study is closely related to a critical examination of the notion of potentiality.

When Jackson said that evolution goes from the simpler to the more complex, from the more organized to the less organized, and the less voluntary to the more voluntary, he was taking a more particularly psychophysiological point of view yet simply drawing upon a number of observations and doctrines from the past. To start with, this means the progressive augmentation of the quantity of neurons, synapses, unitary excitations and inhibitions, and functional summations, with an increase approaching geometrical progression of theoretically possible combinations, the number of which rapidly becoming enormous. In the second place, an increasing mobility of linkages (for Jackson, organization had the sense of rigid structure) which permit the best use of the combinations whose the anatomophysiological aspect was just touched upon. Thirdly, an increasingly rational behavior with all that reason includes of mobility and truthfulness within the whole, i.e., of universality, of liberty in the first sense of the word.[48] Pavlov described another aspect of this evolutionary direction by the notions of temporary connections, of signs of signs, of a second system of signals that allows highest forms of abstraction and generalization without excluding the synthesis and the grasp of concrete reality as such.[49] Teilhard de Chardin saw in evolution a law of complexity-consciousness, or to put it better, of complexity-quality of consciousness, since it is impossible to deny with certainty all consciousness in lower modalities of life simply because, among other reasons, there are more or less distant analogies between other aspects.[50]'

$P = f(G)(E) \ldots$ this is what our teachers tell us. It means that the development of successive behaviors within the phenotype is at the very least a function of the genotype and of the environment. Yet the genotype permits a margin for variations that is not necessarily the same in each case. Perhaps our Nobel prizes for molecular biology have not insisted sufficiently upon the fact that in the prevailing theory the phenotypical explanation is more or less univocal or pluralistic. It is to a greater or lesser extent defined by a genetic script that is supposed to be defined chemically, no matter how sensitive it may be to feedback from the phenotype and the environment, such as functional regulations, induced mutations, and of course Darwinian selection. For example, it is just that which distinguishes an innate behavior from a learned one.

Although it requires a certain degree of inner maturation of the organism, innate behavior demands no preliminary learning; from the start it is adapted to the releasing and satisfaction-giving circumstances in which it was phylogenetically formed. In a way it is delivered "fully assembled" at birth, or at least after a certain maturity happens within the organism. But from the point of view of the individual, this kind of relation is characterized by a marked rigidity and a character that is in a certain fashion extraordinarily partial. It appears to be defined in a univocal fashion by the genetic script, independent of the present variations of the environment, without the least understanding of the whole situation on the part of the subject. Let the sign be detached from its habitual surroundings and the swan will nest on a stone, a robin will attack a bit of red material, and a gosling will follow a boat, or Lorenz, as it would follow its mother. Animals and, doubtless more often than we think, men as well let themselves be deceived by crude decoys as long as they include an innate triggering indicator. The subject is literally a prisoner of a partial element. He is blinded and trapped by it.[51] [52]

The faculty of learning, and, in a sense, even the learned behaviors, are an hereditary ability, a phylogenetic outcome, but not in the sense of a univocal actualization or realization. The subject is able to negotiate the most diverse relations according to circumstances. The relations are increasingly fluid, whether the subject follows the changing situation or explores the given situation. First the orientation, the inquiry, and learning are grafted onto the innate behaviors which they, in a way, extend. The result is a greater margin for individual variation, adaptation, and initiative. The organism searches out situations that release innate instincts and give them satisfaction. It gives variety to these situations through what is called education, a honing and diversifying process, and sets up a calculus of pleasure and pain that is tied to the fulfillment of this kind of instinctual automatism or to its repression. The conditional reflex, or temporary connection, which is subject to fluctuation in principle, is built upon absolute reflex, that is, innate behavior. As Pavlov saw it, *"all of humanity, through the world of signs and signs of signs, (is) out after its daily bread;"* one might add "and a bit of jam as well."

But our species in particular seems to have a kind of detachment. Orientation, learning, investigation, inquiry, knowing . . . all have a tendency to set up relations that are partly detached from the satisfaction of our more primitive instincts. In this sense our reason represents one of our most powerful instincts. Its exercise is accompanied by the most human pleasures, those same for which many of the ancient philosophers reserved the name of happiness.[53] Pavlov, completing his teaching, used to say that the mathematician inclines towards truth as the plant towards light, and he would have been happy to admit, lover and seeker of truth that he himself was, that research gave him a great deal of satisfaction. The thinkers of the Renaissance saw in man a microcosm that attempted, in its own way, to incorporate within itself the macrocosm in order to understand it and in some small way to perfect it. For Christians eternal happiness consists in a vision of God that is one of love, and in a certain sense, of the intellect . . . To return to biology, do we really understand how much in these kinds of activities the phenotype has to be free with respect to a possible defined genetic script?

This does not mean that our other instincts are to be looked down upon; their reasonable satisfaction allows us to enjoy ourselves, to live, and to engage in self-development. Nor does this mean that our learned conducts are immune from becoming rigid; the problem is all one of conservation in development through conservation and emergence, of memory and the formation of good and bad habits. The first can be the surest safeguard of liberty, the second (of which neuroses are simply one case) can be its negation. There is another negation of liberty in the first sense of the word, i.e., a refusal to accept a simple definition from natural history, that of man as a particularly reasonable animal: an excess of blind obedience and the delegation of reason, *"perinde ac cadaver!"* Just as in the preceeding case this tendency is quick to show itself. There are a thousand ways to be the prisoner of a sign, and not only of an innate sign.[54]

Conflicts.

The dialectics of the senses and intelligence, of analysis and synthesis, characterize the progress of thought as it follows the progress of the real and tends to explore it in all of its dimensions. These dialectics are no more devoid of permanent elements than is the whole of reality. They do not coincide completely with each other, nor with the dialectic of contradiction. If you call contradiction the simple difference, then the extension and comprehension of this latter dialectical modality becomes such that it is contained in each of the others or that it contains all of them. But let us leave aside these Byzantine quarrels. Mao Tse-tung reexamined the classic views of Marxism-Leninism, made them more precise and developed them. His recommendation was to start by studying concrete situations, to neglect no part of them, to look at the whole rather than the part and to pick out the essential. In this he showed himself a good naturalist as well as a good mathematician. We might also say that he makes use of the most classic form of dialectic in order to understand the dialectic of contradiction. In a sense the latter would contain the former and at the same time be a fundamental moving principle.[55] We are going to see in a few concrete examples, at least two of which are relatively familiar to us, that it is not always easy to say who are the partners in the struggle, how an internal contradiction is delimited, or what is the meaning of the so-called contradictory relation.

Hegel opposes and at the same time identifies the rose and the rose-bud in the sense of the identity of contraries. He proceeds in a more or less contradictory fashion from the formal logic point of view to a more or less arbitrary partitioning in a unitary process, an original and relational process, and then opposes and unifies among themselves these more or less artificially contrived parts. This example was proposed by Hegel himself and has been frequently cited, but it is not necessarily one that holds up in all cases. Furthermore the process, the development, the direction of the change would verify the principle of identity, but as applied to movement.[56] In the class struggle the antagonist contradiction would be at the heart of the whole that is constituted by the two classes in question and would characterize their relations. In the Darwinian and Neodarwinian theories (attractive theories but with many unresolved difficulties) the struggle would be between the organism and its environment.[57] The two or three antagonist factors at stake would be heredity, chance mutations in the sense of causal series that are in some way independent, and selection. Through their numerical importance and their variety in large populations and on the geological time ladder, chance mutations would literally constitute the material of evolution, so to speak, like a block of marble. Fitness, the greatest fitness of the relations between the changed organism and its environment, and also that of the internal relations, would constitute the criterion of selection, like the sculptor and his chisel: to be adapted, better adapted, or not to be. Let us take note in passing that this principle goes beyond Darwin's theory.[58]

Let us observe further that in this theory, except in the case of a precociously lethal mutation, the judgement of fit relation, of appropriate agreement, passed by the whole on its parts is one that is made in relatively advanced stages of the phenotypical development of the organism bearing and eventually perpetuating the mutated genotype. Consequently there is a retroactivity at work here, i.e., feedback. P. P. Grassé, a former teacher of ours, provides an excellent treatment of some of these problems.[59]

Obstacles, whether exterior, interior, or interiorized, can have a destructive relationship with us, one that stops progress, or one that causes us to regress. Yet they can move us either to destroy them, surmount them, turn them about, set them aside, or even change our aims. Normal and pathological psychoanalysis shows us the importance of conflict resolution in our normal development and the neurotic arrested development resulting from lack of resolution and fixations. Think for a moment about the consequences of the conflicts we are prey to: those between our different drives, innate or acquired; those between our defenses and instinctive behavior which is judged, either consciously or inconsciously, to be against current or introjected injunctions of our parents or group, inadequate for the situation, or contrary to the authentic rationality of the self, with all the processes of repression, condensation, relational modification, displacement, sublimation, and so forth. We might take a fresh look at how important for becoming an adult are the projects that a child devises to surmount his littleness, his weakness, his inferiority in his early conflicts more or less mixed with friendship, with his peers, parents, teachers, and the vast world . . .[60] [61] The combat, with all of its positive effects, continues as long as life itself. Our penchant towards universality and freedom is itself marked by struggle from beginning to end: that between rigid, partial relation, and movement within the whole, which is a condition of greater understanding and enlightened behavior; partially interior combats of the person in situation, in relation, spiritual struggles . . .

If we affirm the internal character of a contradiction, in the sense of a struggle or combat or antagonist contradiction, and also of the identity of contraries, we are first of all highlighting a certain unity of the real, an authentic originality, a real dialectical level independent of the knowledge relationship that we form or set about to form with it. We have discussed this at the beginning of this work. It is perhaps less difficult to outline wholes at the interior of which original realities are in a combat relation. As to knowing if we are dealing with the realization of what was virtual, with an actualization of potencies, when new reality arises from the combat, we direct the reader to the note on potency.[62]

Part Three
Theory of Development

A *Knowledge of Development and Development of Knowledge*

1   *Knowledge as Conscious Modification of a Subject in Relation*

Knowledge: a process common to two terms in relationship, a function not of knowledge itself but of reality and the subject's aptitude to know.
In the preceding studies, knowledge emerged as a relationship and as an aspect.[63] More precisely, it is a conscious aspect of a process that is unfolding in a subject in relation, the growth of a conscious relationship. *Cum gnoscere:* knowledge as a common action. Knowledge, said Aristotle, is an act common to reality that is generally knowable and to a subject that, after its own fashion, is able to know. In an analogous sense, the wave is an act common to the stone and the water. This definition is an excellent one in more than one respect, but it is linked to the theory of potency and act, matter and form, and the intellectual soul and the body, which is less than completely defensible.[64]

What is potency, after all? A simple truism stating that if an event occured it was able to occur? An illusory projection backward? Is it a virtuality of the part or of the whole? Does it contain only one possible future or several? Is it a necessity or does it involve the ability to say no? Is it a creativity that makes prediction impossible? Further, virtuality is sometimes confused with the material element, in the sense of a brick or an atom. In this sense it is true that, to the extent that the subject becomes conscious of it, a luminous, i.e., illuminated object "loses its matter along the way" if not its effects: initially, its "condensed matter," and then, after its consequences have gone beyond the physical plane of eyesight, its radiant or reflected energy distributed in vibrations and quanta. The nervous system then begins to react and, in its own way, to transmit: as the Ancients put it, the thing known is in the subject in a way proper to the subject. As to act and form, they would have the disadvantage of artificially stopping change and affording only instantaneous, intermittent, and static glimpses of it.

Rather than common act, we prefer to speak in terms of common process.

Or still better of mathematical function. The new point of view is that of process, of the progression of knowledge following its own movement and the movement of the real. Some new precisions are necessary, particularly in the definition of what we have called the two terms of the relation. What is related, and to what?

When scrutinizing reality, the subject begins by centering his interest and attention, by focusing the projector and determining the operational field. What frequently happens is that the first term of the relation is reduced to the field determined by the subject, and this field is called "object." As a consequence, expressions such as object relation, relation between subject and object are used, which obscure the problem somewhat since the object depends in part upon the subject and is partially subjective. In fact, the object belongs exclusively to neither of the two terms, but rather to both at once or, more exactly, to their relationship. It constitutes a first analytic and synthetic modality of the latter. Like all our subsequent analytic and synthetic activity, this first centering is not necessarily arbitrary. Just as much as a simple artifice or a puzzle effect, it can be founded upon reality and correspond to preexistent cleavage planes between real originalities or interior to them. It frequently does not modify the first term.

This is not the case in some other examination procedures; particle physics, chemical analysis, anatomical dissection, psychoanalysis, etc., cannot help us to know reality without at the same time introducing some kind of change in it. More than the objectal focalization that does not really modify the first term of the knowledge relation, there are facts of a like order which might lead us to declare that reality is not knowable because it has to be modified to be known. Suffice it to observe that there are several approaches; granted that all of them really modify the reality to be known, they do not all do so in the same fashion. In the final analysis, none of these modifications is retroactive: in the worst hypothesis, thought remains generally able to reconstruct the past.

Briefly, the first term of the relation called knowledge is the *res universa* of Cicero, Kant's thing-in-itself relieved of its incommunicability, reality as it is in itself independently of being known. This means that the knowledge relation is not in relation with itself, that the function is not one of itself, but that it touches upon reality. The second term is the subject, an existing concrete individual. Its capacity to know varies according to species, individual, age, and circumstances. Knowledge takes place in each subject under the mode proper to the subject, and at the same time under a common mode. On the whole, man is more able to understand than an animal, an adult more than an infant, a civilized person more than a savage, the wise man more than the ignorant one, one who has practical experience more than one who has not, the free man more than the enslaved one, one who has some leisure more than one who is crushed under an inhuman burden. This makes the notion of function more precise without changing the definition of the two terms: the conscious process which takes place within the second term at contact with the first is a function of the latter as well as of the aptitude of the subject to know.

This is not to say that the subject is unable to know itself or its peers, or that the human sciences in general, and the theory of knowledge in particular, are any more a prey to subjectivity and the obscuring effect of the projection of knowledge's shadow upon reality than are the other sciences. Even when one listens to one's own life, as in Bergsonian intuition, a didactic psychoanalysis, an examination of conscience, or a spiritual exercise, there remains a difference of one degree of reflection between the two terms of the relation.

Elements common to the two terms of the relation and to each of the aspects, degrees and modalities of the psychophysiological modifications of the subject. The transmission of the common element through the successive steps of the act of consciousness.
Knowledge is characterized by elements common to the two terms of the relation and to each of the aspects, degrees, and modalities of the psychophysiological modifications of the subject, from sensation to the most sophisticated forms of intelligence. A few of these common elements have been listed in the first two parts of this work. Several of them are of the temporal order; this observation will be taken up again and developed with regard to the knowledge of change and of the absence of change. They characterize the transformation, the effect of the first term developing in the subject, the common process of both terms within the second, the function which, all else being equal regarding the subject's aptitude to know, links the modification within the subject to that which is other than that modification. They are transmitted through the different stages of the act of consciousenss, guaranteeing that at each of them, despite their proper differences, knowledge does not feed upon itself at some given level, nor does some higher, posterior level of knowledge touch upon a lower, prior level only: if C is a function of B, and B is a function of A, then C is a function of A. [65] [66] [67] [68] [69]

At each degree of mental modification, the transmitted common element rising into consciousness is referred to the first term in an immediate and nonreflective way. The realism of knowledge is affirmed implicitly as well as the correspondence, the law of transformation, the function that links the mental modification to a reality other than itself. This affirmation signals a community of origin and stands as a sign and a condition of the relations between the part and the whole. It does not mean that knowledge is immune from illusion, error, insufficiency, limitations, or illness. It involves no notional definition of common elements, several of which, indeed, remain undefinable or *sui generis,* such as identity, difference, simultaneity, etc. This affirmation is, however, formed, verified and maintained in relation, by relation, for relation, and is proved by practice, general consensus, and by the *reductio ad absurdum;* the consequences are what tell us about the value of the implicit affirmation of correspondence, and they teach us about truth and error, both as to notion and to application.

Some of the preceding remarks are equally true for the biological, reactional levels that occur before consciousness. Presence, absence, the moment, repetition, the rhythm of blinking eyelids and the reflex action of the pupils in response to alternating light and darkness, these have already constituted an affirmation of correspondence and serve as a practical judgment about the first term, even before neural modifications have begun to touch areas of the brain whose activation sparks the most primitive forms of consciousness. But before the slightest organic change, the photoelectric cell and electronic recorders have already made an analogous judgment about the changes of intensity of light.

Men have no exclusivity in this matter. Everything else that exists, animals, vegetables, inanimate bodies whether made by the hand of man or not, each in a different way affirms, consciously or unconsciously, implicitly or explicitly, that if everything else is equal in their particular ability to know, to react, to respond, to distinguish and discern, then a like cause produces a like effect within themselves. All, therefore, can judge reality in an identical sense. In the event of a collision, the driver, passengers, the dog, the child, passers-by, the car, and the causeway, all bear the same witness. What stands out here is the common domain of the parts relating within the whole, the reciprocal adaptation, logic, truth, commensurability among things, conservation in the improvement of knowing, as well as in the development of the real in general. The originality proper to each level constitutes another aspect of reality.

A return to Kant and phenomenology. Neither knowledge nor the theory of knowledge are separated from the real. They are not tautological and they do not involve a displacement of the problem.

"All knowledge is but a phenomenology, an intellectual and subjective categorization of subjective sense phenomena. What things are in themselves is unknown to us. We know only our way of knowing, according to the pure a priori *categories of intelligence and the pure* a priori *forms of sensibility. Intelligence is ultimately related to sensibility. Space and time are pure* a priori *forms of sensibility. Remove the subject, and relations in accordance with the categories, as well as space and time, simply disappear."*[70]

Such, in brief, is the theory of Kant and the phenomenologists.[71] It has the merit of recalling to mind that we do not coincide with what we know, and of drawing attention to the importance, within the relation, of the related subject, and to the fact that knowledge depends as well upon our aptitude to know and our manner of knowing. Otherwise, however, it seems to be profoundly erroneous. Indeed, to know is not to coincide with what is known, but that does not lead to the further conclusion that the knower is separated from the known. To know is to enter into a relation.

Far from obfuscating reality behind the succesive and superimposed "screens" of the senses and intelligence, knowledge enlightens it. Knowledge involves identities and differences between the two terms of the relation, and between the different moments, levels, and modalities of the second term, that is, of the knowing subject. The differences signal originality and emergence. The common elements point up the community of origin, belonging, conservation, and commensurability. They permeate the relation from "head to toe," so to speak, with various outcomes. They are observable not only in the "longitudinal" sense, that for example of psycho-physics and psychophysio-physics, but even in the "transversal" sense of psychophysiology. They belong to the temporal order as well, and that means that knowledge of real development, of change and absence of change, is not an *a priori* form of sensibility, that such a knowledge brings into play all the degrees of knowing according to both their proper and common modalities, and touches reality without any coessential distortion.

Knowledge, therefore, is not directed back upon itself. It is separated from reality by no opaque screen, whether sensorial, phenomenal, or intellectual, categorial. The truth of our judgments, the correction of our logical mechanisms, the validity as to the notion and application of principles of thought that are otherwise *sui generis* and indefinable, are proved by the analogous and partially common behavior of numerous diverse systems placed in the same circumstances, by general consensus, by practice, by consequences, and by the absurd. Knowledge about knowledge, the "theory of knowledge," offers no particular difficulty: as we have already said, there is a difference of one degree of reflection between the two terms in relation. Certainly the theorist who considers knowledge should, as well as the subject whose relation he is studying, know the first term of that relation in order to explain the law of correspondence, the notions of function and elements common to the two terms of the relation. But this is no shifting of the problem, nor is there any kind of circle here. Indeed, both the knowing subject and the scientist who studies him know reality independently of each other, and for each of them the preceding validations are valuable separately.

The dialectic of concrete thought. Sense and intelligence. Analysis and synthesis. Analogical knowledge. The tendency towards universality.

An ancient philosophical approach reduces abstraction to sophisticated, intellectual modalities of thought, and strips it from sensibility; it opposes the latter to intelligence and considers that opposition to be between concrete and abstract thought. Since Parmenides and Heraclitus, numerous philosophers have believed that permanence was discovered or invented by intellectual thought, confused with abstract thought, while change could be grasped only by experience and sense intuition, confused with concrete thought.[72] This lacks exactness in more than one respect.

Concrete, from *cum crescere, concrescere*, to meet each other, to grow with, first means full and entire reality, then our tendency to know reality always more and more completely, in more and more ways, and under more and more aspects, all the time holding on to our own originality and remaining distinct. Concrete thought is consequently synonymous with complete thought, and for that reason concrete thought is fundamentally synthetic. But the opposition that sometimes is made between concrete and abstract thought ought not allow us to forget that there is no mental synthesis without analysis, and that the analytical data that precede the synthesis and prepare for them constitute so many new points of view about reality. Analysis and synthesis are two aspects of concrete thought, two aspects among others. There is no opposition here unless we take the part for the whole.

Ab trahere, to take from: to abstract means to analyze. The senses are above all analytical. Knowledge begins with sense analysis, continuing through more and more sophisticated modalities of thought. These modalities differ but conserve elements that they have in common with the first term of the relation and between themselves: gnosia, word, judgment, etc. These later, succesive modalities are often called intellectual. They contain more of the synthetic, but are not wholly without analytical aspects. To the extent that it abstracts more or less from differences, analytic thought is more or less general, more or less applicable to classes and to wholes that are more or less vast, and this is valid for all levels and modalities of analysis. The generality of sensorial analysis differs qualitatively from intellectual abstraction, and not quantitatively: for instance, the sensation of in-compenetrability of bodies from the atomic theory.

It would be paradoxical to maintain that concrete thought, which seeks to know reality in the most complete way possible, is less universally applicable than analytical thought because it takes into account differences rather than abstracts from them, as does the latter. First of all, the tendency towards universality is the tendency to understand the universe more and more completely. Far from being opposed to analysis, concrete thought contains it.

No matter how thorough knowledge may be, it is not possible to know everything, nor is it possible to know in all possible ways at the same time. Succession is the rule between different degrees of knowledge, rather than simultaneity, and the same applies to different kinds of knowledge at each degree of knowledge. Concrete thought unfolds in time. It has its own proper movement by which it reviews the real in successive stages. Its dialectic contains analytic and synthetic dialectic as well as that of the senses and intelligence [73]

With the notion of aspects, of reuniting in the mind that which is one in reality but can be separated by the mind initially, we are face to face with one of the principal modalities of analytic and synthetic dialectic. Another of its modalities consists in the oscillation of thought between the analysis of an area that is common to processes that are otherwise different, and the statement that each of these processes, when it is considered apart and with its proper particularities, does truly embrace the common area and, in its own way, satisfies the common law. This attribution constitutes the synthetic movement. It is a movement of thought that has been termed, in a less than happy way it seems, "analogical abstraction" or, in short, synthetic analysis. The air of contradiction surrounding this expression, in the formal logic sense, stems from the fact that the two successive moments are not distinguished. It is doubtless better to say that it is characteristic of analogical knowledge, which constitutes one of the most fundamental mechanisms of thought. The latter has innumerable applications in all of the areas of the real and all levels of knowledge. They are found in the most elementary reactions as well as in the most sophisticated symbolism of conversation, art, science, dreams, and neuroses. They are found in financial exchange from barter to the use of money, in numeration as well as in axiomatic notations almost entirely stripped of sense representations, in the knowledge of being as well as in that of Being, or God, at least according to some theologians and philosophers.[74]

The development of the faculty of knowing, of knowledge as such and of the different kinds of knowledge, the increasingly complete, concrete, and universal character of practical and theoretical awareness, serve to characterize the development of the discrete knowledge process, as well as the development of species, individuals, societies, and civilizations. They are observed empirically, but they seem to have the weight of necessity. They signify differentiation and unification, the increase in originality as well as the improvement of the mutual agreement of parts in relations within the whole, the growth of truth, logic, and consciousness. The behaviors of reciprocal adaptation, which are logical and true in a certain sense, are initially unconscious. Little by little, through biological and human development, the part grows in consciousness of the whole, and reality (Hegel might better have limited himself to that expression) becomes conscious of itself.[75] Other lines of evolution emerge, however, such as the tendency to delegate reason, to abandon one's powers of self-information, self-deliberation and self-decision, and yield them to others.

2 *Knowledge of Change and of the Absence of Change*

Development involves change and absence of change. Despite its etymology, it has lost its sense of univocal explicitation and implies no stance regarding the notion of virtuality. Its knowledge yields to a deployment of temporal notions that are more or less grounded in reality, linking up with the notions of identity, difference, and originalities in relation: process, duration, intermittence, enduring identity or permanence or the absence of change, intermittent identity or repetition, change, simultaneity that is more or less enduring, nonsimultaneity or succession, order of succession, before, during, after, past, present, future, instantaneousness, moment either in the mathematical sense or in the dialectical sense, interval of time, progress, leap, stage, evolution, revolution . . . As are identity and difference, the temporal determinations in us and in things are *sui generis*, unique in their genera, and undefinable even analogically. One might almost speak of them in terms of "principles" and "categories" of the real, and of real thought really joined to the real. The philosopher was right who proved movement by walking. Though they are *sui generis* in concept, they are no less observable, case by case, measurable, calculable, demonstrable, predictable, etc., depending on the individual case. And as the behaviors of other biological and physical systems indicate we are not the only observers.

Simultaneity, succession, temporal interval.
Simultaneity characterizes a confrontation between processes that are changing or unchanging. It is more or less enduring, and not reducible to a mathematical moment or instant, except by way of a fiction as described below. Succession and the order of succession can depend upon this confrontation—before, during, or after the encounter between two processes—or it can be seen within a given process. An interval of time is also involved in both instances, whether in the case of two successive

encounters between different processes, or two successive events in the same process. The observer chooses the most convenient reference, often an astronomic clock, chronometer, or watch.

Einstein felt that events simultaneous in one system of spatial references might not be so in another system that was moving in respect to the first, but that the differences could not be picked up by our instruments of measure except in cases where the displacement speeds were close to the speed of light. Experience would show that the speed of the latter within a void is constant no matter what movement there may be in respect to the source and the receiver, but it also would show that, correlatively to these relative movements, distances and temporal intervals vary. As a result we have a physical theory that would be at once more simple and more comprehensive. It appeals to a lesser number of conceptual starting points, would explain even the most difficult observations, lends itself to prediction, and includes without destroying, as a particular case, the older theory of mechanics that gave birth to it.[76] [77]

Duration. Thought and movement according to Bergson. Identity of contraries and struggle between contraries in Hegel.

Duration involves noninterruption or nonintermittence, permanence, change, or permanence and change together. An identity passes for being more or less durable through comparison with changes.

Bergson's philosophy of duration, it would seem, offers both acceptable and unacceptable concepts. He equates duration with change purified of all permanence, repetition, and identity; for him it is perpetual creation stripped of all virtuality, predetermination, and predictability. He makes of it the very substance of consciousness and spirit. For him the two are reduced to one, and he reifies them, so to speak, separating them, as constantly changing reality, from a body that is subject to repetition. This does not prevent him from having the body penetrated by spirit, seeming thus to oscillate between a dualism of separation and noncorrespondence and a monistic panspiritualism. Duration and change are indivisible. When someone such as Zeno attempts to divide them, it can be demonstrated that Achilles cannot overtake the tortoise. They can only be grasped intuitively and concretely, by listening to one's own life. Intelligence is meant for fabrication, for transitive, exterior action; it makes artificial breaks. The moments of mathematics do not exist. Utility is the only reason that the past is distinguished from the present, and that distinction, moreover, is quite variable. Real succession, however, is not denied.[78]

In our opinion duration characterizes reality, one and diverse, permanent and changing, exterior or interior, knowable under several aspects that are reducible to the real unity of concrete beings. Concrete knowledge, knowledge that is the most complete and synthetic possible, contains abstraction and analysis as well. The vision of continuous evolution among living beings is grounded upon stratigraphy; the acts of awareness and transference arise from intermittent psychoanalytical sessions; the symphony is a collection of musical notes.

The whole can be divided into different processes, and there can be division within a single process according to determinations of a temporal nature: moments in the dialectical sense of the word, levels, critical points, sudden transformations, momentary accelerations of change, etc. Such divisions bring with them the risk of artificiality, even though they can be firmly grounded in reality. Bergson was insistent on the first point of view. Hegel himself, in his famous example of dialectic, seems to oscillate between affirming that the flower and the fruit constitute real unities and that they are no more than fictitious conventions. The negation of each of these moments by the following, the struggle between contraries, these are basically derived from the viewpoint of the succession of states; from the perspective of the undivided process considered as a whole we have the identification of contraries.[79]

The weakness of the opposition between the philosophies of permanence and the philosophies of change.

Sometimes one is tempted to think that philosophy uses two different methods, one of them more intuitive and closer to the senses, the other more intellectual and abstract. With the first we would understand change, with the second the absence of change. In the West, Heraclitus and Parmenides represent the respective origins of these two currents of thought. Different ages have given rise to various attempts at synthesizing the two.

Take the case of Plato. Is not his great distinction between the world of sense, at once in motion and a little illusory, and the intelligible world, that of the ideas purified of all change, immutable and eternal, a case in point? And the same applies to a number of Christian philosophers, whether Aristotelian-thomist or Aristotelian-platonist, who separate the philosophy of nature from ontology, the science of being as such. The first, since it would not achieve the degree of analogical abstraction of the second, would look to that which changes, "generation and corruption," while the second would seize the immutable source of things in their relation to the Immutable Prime Mover, Being, He whose name is "I am," He who is known as God. In addition to a reversal of Hegelian platonism or pantheism, do we not have in Engels the exact opposite of preceding opinions as he absorbs philosophy into the dialectic of nature, makes of the latter the science of change, and anathematizes metaphysics as fraught with illusions such as immobility, eternity, and the supernatural, and as a purveyor of true opiates and artifical paradises?[80] And, with a touch of pessimism regarding our knowing faculties, is not this the opinion of Kant that reduces time to a phenomenal opaqueness, to an *a priori* form of sensibility? And does not Bergson take intelligence, particularly abstract intelligence, and make it the place where "realities" are fictitious fractions and immobilizations? Does he not accord to intuition alone the power to know the changing substance of spiritual reality, always new, discordant with the world of the body, or, on the contrary, penetrating and transforming it?

For us every philosophy, every science, all knowing, every relationship even unconscious, even nonbiological, touches upon reality. In this reality, we hold, both real change and the real absence of change are known through all our ways of knowing, from the most humble to the most sophisticated, each moment, degree, and modality of knowing dictating its proper manner. Each of these moments, degrees and modalities, from sensation and even from preconscious reactions to the most evolved forms of intelligence, in our opinion seems to contain analysis, i.e., abstraction, and synthesis, i.e., setting up relationships or attributing to concrete individual subjects or to classes.

Laws: permanent or transitory, general or special.

We do not know how long the world has endured, how long it will endure, whether it had a beginning or whether it will have an end, if it depends on an immutable, uncreated Being having neither beginning nor end, or even whether these words make sense . . . Some think that such inquiries either have or will receive an answer based upon scientific certitudes. Others, consciously or unconsciously, explicitly or implicitly, give answer in terms of faith, a faith that is more or less grounded on motives of credibility or lack of credibility. We presume that if there is life in the universe elsewhere than upon earth, and if the universe had a beginning, then life did not begin until afterwards. We know that life appeared on earth some millions of years after the latter was formed and that other living organisms preceded man on earth.

We can compare the periods of time involved, those of an individual, a society, species, or a star. We speak relatively when we say a process lasts a short time or a long time: *the roses live but the time of a morning . . ."*

It is with these reservations and precisions that we can begin to attempt descriptions of modalities of reality that are permanent or more or less enduringly unchangeable: general laws, laws that are valid for all reality in the world and which embrace its duration, indicating conservation, identity, analogy, and common domain—and special laws valid only for a certain level of evolution and limited to its duration, laws that focus upon difference and emergence and which define more or less limited groups of identical or like individuals.

But what about the laws that we claim to discover? Are they not forever changing with the progress of science? Is it not true to say that, in affirming the existence of permanent or steadfastly unchanging modalities of the real, we presume that the future is determined univocally and quite predictable? If the most enduring is at the same time of the broadest commonality, surpassing differences, originalities, levels of evolution, embracing all reality in the universe from its beginning to its end, or eternally, does this not take us back to the old hierarchy of knowledge according to the triple criterion, the threefold gradation of abstraction, generality, and immutability? For the moment let us limit ourselves to recall that evolution and revolutions of thought, like those of the reality in general that they impact and of which they form a part, are not always the result of a pure and simple annihilation of that which precedes, but that they might also be the result of conservation and emergence.[81] Consider analytic and synthetic dialectic, the synthesis of aspects that were intitially grasped as separated realities and not as aspects at all.

The permanence of the principle of identity. Its degree of universality. The way in which it applies to change.

The principle of identity is without doubt one of the most universal and enduring laws of reality. This is so even though its understanding can diminish in us as our relationship with the real weakens and we are partially isolated and disinserted, as in dreams. To be sure, in order to verify it a number of the ancient philosophers have relied upon what may be called *flashes,* or instantaneous glimpses of a change in process. Bergson reminds us that no matter how brief the interval of time between two such glimpses, their sum will not reconstitute the real change, even though admitting that these theoretical "slices" do not amount to the concrete nonexistence of mathematical moments or points. When we were discussing Bergson and Kant, however, we said that to know is not the same as to coincide with or to be separated from, that even the grasp we have of our interior development differs from it by one degree of reflection, and that these two facts by no means detract from a basic realism of knowledge. As for Hegel, he assigned different meanings to these instants, either simultaneously or at successive times. He judged them to be at once artificial, giving us the identification of contraries, and grounded in reality, which gives us the opposition of contraries.

Whether we grasp an uninterrupted, concrete duration, a growing that includes both change and the absence of change, or, in such processes, only intermittent slices in time that are more or less instantaneous or contiguous with each other, it seems to us that the two procedures are not mutually exclusive but that they complement and shed light upon each other. Both, individually and in consort, show not only the identity of the changeless, but in a certain way and within certain limits they show the identity of change.

What has happened has happened. The past escapes change. It is immutable, and along with it all that has reference to it, such as memory. As for the future, the identity of change can be understood in two ways. The one is clear and certain, the other obscure and full of doubt. One can either say that future reality will be what it will be, no matter whether the present reality contains many "possible" futures or not, or affirm the univocal predetermination of what is to come. In all cases, past and present change, at least what pertains to that versant of the present which is already the legacy of the past, is defined really and is susceptible of identification. Even if it was not univocally predetermined in advance, future change becomes defined and identifiable to the extent that it comes to be. In other words, it seems to us that the principle of identity is verified in realized change, change in the process of realization, and change in so far as it will be realized, but that we should set aside the question of unicity or multiplicity of what is virtual in the part and in the whole. If it is true that Socrates was born, lived, taught, was condemned, drank the hemlock and died, it is true for all time. The path was unique. But does this mean that no other paths were possible?

Among the ways by which a change is characterized is its direction. This can be either changing or unchanging. We can speak of it as we did of change in general: it is univocally defined and identified as such to the extent that the change that it characterizes has been realized, is being realized, or will be realized. But this does not necessarily mean that it is predetermined nor, *a fortiori,* that it is predictable.

There are innumerable examples of identity and identification of the changing or unchanging direction of a change. The laws of physics, biological, social, historical, and dialectical laws describe these characteristics of the growth of the real, predict them, or strive to do so. Originality and relationship, the increase of reciprocal adaptation, of truth, logic, consciousness, and the mutual enrichment within differentiation and unification, these constitute some of the major constants in biological and human development in so far as it involves both the lack of change and change that takes place according to an unchanging direction. But we also see examples of deviations, of regressions, annihilations, and other evolutionary lines, and here again we run up against the question of determination or indetermination, of predictability, of the creation of the future.

Some examples of physical, biological, and human permanence, repetitions, changes, rhythms and tempos.

Various organic activities that are repetitive, cyclical, and periodic, have been called, not without reason, biological clocks. Examples of these would be the cardiac, respiratory, alimentary, excretory, and menstrual rhythms, the more or less regular alternance between waking and sleeping, exertion and rest, work and recreation, desire and satisfaction. . . .[82]

But this notion covers but a small fraction of our development. The latter includes as well rhythms and tempos which are neither repetitive, periodic, nor cyclical. These might be better compared to a sandglass than to a clock. There is man's average lifespan, which has been slightly increased in the last century or two with the progress of medicine. There are the stages of our growth and decline—infancy, adolescence, maturity, and old age—until now accelerated or decelerated by exterior factors in only a small proportion. There are psychophysiological tempos, which cover the neural time periods of axonal conduction and synapses, increasing with the number of neurons and the intervention of peripheral elements that are relatively inert, such as the muscles, etc. . . . Sensation, nonverbal recognition, and the word arise successively at about a few tenths of a second intervals during the half second which follows the stimulation.[83] Inner speech, also called verbal thought or the mental word, which some of the ancient philosophers considered the least physical of our activiites, under normal circumstances or in case of a peripheral neuromotor slowdown, takes place at about the same speed as the word spoken aloud, an indication that a large part of the nerve circuits are common to both.[84]

There is nothing particularly astonishing about the observation that there is a certain proportionality between human and biological rhythms and those of the whole of reality: it is the condition and sign of our existing and being a part of the real. As in the case of all biological conduct and every phenotype, this temporal proportionality between the individual and his environment would be more or less strictly defined by the genetic code. It would also be bequeathed to each individual by phylogenesis, by past confrontation, whether in the "innate" sense, strictly and rigidly preadapted, or under the form of a learning capacity. The two are not necessarily exclusive of each other, yet are able to coexist, fit together, and complete each other in variable proportions. Richelle ventures the hypothesis of a phylogenetic improvement of temporal regulations in the sense of a relative increase of learning aptitudes.[85] The word hypothesis is possibly a little weak. Though we believe less and less in astrology, astronomy continues to regulate gardens and gardeners, and the sun rules a good number of our relations, albeit in these times through the intermediary of a watch.

When, at the heart of a species, a group perceives or invents rhythms that were hitherto unknown, the group's survival can depend upon their use, lack of use, or misuse. The expansion or death of the group can be at stake, whether physical or spiritual, and also that of the group's members and those with whom they are in relations. It is important to grasp the meaning of the criteria, to know how to select them and order them. As much if not more than others, the educator, spiritual director, and the physician should be attentive to our rhythms. The Benedictine bell and the outward regularity at the office rule the interior perfection of the monks and their progress in what they believe to be the knowledge and love of God, progress towards eternal life.[86] Not even the most brutal taskmaster can accelerate beyond measure the cadence of the assembly line, nor that of the astounding machine putting food into the mouth of Charlie Chaplin in "Modern Times." "For better or for worse," we are beginnning to have at our disposal automation, virtually instantaneous means of communication, computers that function at a millionth of a second, while our own synapses take a tenth of a second . . . Perhaps one of the most urgent tasks facing us is that of disassociating human time from that of the machine, or adapting the latter to man and making it serve human time. It is a task of enabling man and his time to expand and be enriched through technology. But freeing man from the time card and inhuman rhythms is perhaps not equivalent to supressing punctuality in respect to oneself and others, which is a royal gesture of politeness.[87]

Human development demands a certain choosing, a certain ordering and subordination of rhythms and tempos. It requires that we be neither harassed nor scattered, and that we have a modicum of well being, free time, and tranquility of the spirit.[88]

3 *Determination, Indetermination,*
Prediction, Creation of the Future

A little more history.
Furthermore the analysis of change has given way to a series of other notions more or less based on reality, involving all manner of crossed lines, derivations, and erosions of meaning: being, nonbeing, degrees of reality, virtuality, potency that is more or less passive *(possibilitas, Möglichkeit)*, an "other" receiving the imprint of the Idea like wax, or "desiring the form as the female desires the male," matter or potency that is more or less primary, more or less close to realization, material cause, elements, body, active potency *(potentia)*, agent, entelechy, act, form, intellectual soul dispensing with corporeal concomitants, formal cause, essence, Idea, pure Act, Prime Unmoved Mover, God, secondary, primary, and final causes, Alpha and Omega, contradiction, combat, etc. . . . The Megarians, Tricot tells us, "profess an absolute necessitarianism;"[89] for them the unfolding of the whole is determined in advance, a little like in the mosaic egg of the embryologists,[90] or in Hartsoecher's *homonculus*. Bergson inclines towards the indetermination of the spiritual future, and therefore towards its nonpredictability. Where the latter is concerned he makes of the notion of potency an illusory retroactivity, abandons the domain of matter and body to repetition, and only by having the world of the body penetrated by the spirit does he save his doctrine from a dualism of noncorrespondence, of shattering . . . In the texts of Bergson it is difficult not to perceive an echo of Aristotle, who conferred on rational powers alone the potentiality of contraries and limited irrational powers to a single effect.

Illusory or not, well or badly posed, these are the old problems of the self and the other, of the old and the new, of determinism, creative evolution, human liberty, project, scientific predictability, divine foreknowledge . . . Perhaps because of their generality and because of a certain common conformation to reality, the great questions and approaches are relatively restrained in number. The majority of philosophies have a certain air of kinship. For its part, modern science claims to limit itself to the domain of efficient causality, correlations, and functions, not to mention properties. There are, nevertheless, few previous notions, questions and theories that are completely foreign to it.

The fact of scientific prediction seems to be in contradiction with the Aristotelian idea that virtuality is unknowable before its actualization. Aristotle, it seems, attempted to resolve or lessen this difficulty by saying that potency can be known before the act in cases of repetition. The argument is clearly tautological: what is actually foreseen is the repetition, what is affirmed is the repetition in potency. The weakness of this argument is easily seen through an example frequently used in the Aristotelian tradition, that of biological generation: reproduction and specific heredity were known and therefore "predicted," but not the evolution of the species. On the contrary, when Thomas Aquinas wrote *"rationes autem futurorum possunt esse universales, et intellectu perceptibiles: et de eis etiam possunt esse scientiae,"*[91] that meant that scientific prediction on the basis of empirical observation, logico-mathematical necessity, and understanding of the profound laws of reality were already known.[92]

Empiricism, necessity, abstraction, and concretude in scientific prediction.

Empirical prediction extrapolates a repetitive or enduring identity, or a stable direction, an unchanging orientation of change. They are simply observed but their profound necessity is not seen. As for logical necessity, it is clearly a property common to the part and the whole. It develops itself within us through contact with the real. It is a summary of experiences. It wanes under various circumstances, and notably in certain kinds of isolation and sensory deprivation. It allows others sorts of isolation, such as mathematical reasoning. This latter, as it serves to predict the future, brings about an interior summary of the change. It looks to the observed premises, abandons them provisionally, and then proceeds, so to speak, in the direction towards which they point, taking into consideration both their proper characteristics and common logic. If the premises are correctly observed, true and sufficient, and if the reasoning is well done and the process under study is determined univocally, then the logical consequences are true and the prediction verifiable.

It is customary to hold that the progress of scientific theories is in direct relation with that of observation and that of the logico-mathematical apparatus. The more the real process is determined, the observation has breadth and detail, the objects of the observation are well chosen, the logic has rigor, and the mathematical vehicles are adapted, the greater is the certainty of prediction. The development of science and its power of prediction involves suppression, conservation, and emergence. A theory that was originally considered general can become a particular case of a theory that is still more general. Prediction can only discern the broad outlines of the future, allowing for a certain real indetermination, the interventions of chance, or our own ignorance of detail. There are some real logical necessities without correspondence in the rest of concrete reality, a little like saying that essence can be derived from existence, but not vice-versa. If logic is originally ordered towards reciprocal adaptation and the mutual agreement of terms in relation, in a sense towards the truth of the relationship, it can, at least at some times, place itself at the service of error or falsehood: the mechanisms of reason remain the same even though the premises are insufficient or untrue.

We must not forget, however, that in its search for completeness, concreteness and universality, thought is not reducible to analysis, no matter how generalizing the latter may be, nor to synthesis, but that it involves movement between both poles. Further, that logico-mathematical abstraction is not the only form of analysis, and that logic itself arises from and is sustained by experience. Lastly, that not everything is demonstrable, starting with the principles of logic and their foundations in the whole of reality.

Additionally, it is often equivalent to speak of a common characteristic as more general and more enduring than differences insofar as it is observed as constant through successive emergences and differentiations. Is this extrapolation any less problematical? Who can prove that laws now considered to be general and enduring will continue to be valid? Who would make certain very long term predictions resulting from the second principle of thermodynamics, its conditions of application, and its apparent exceptions? From the biological tendency towards differentiation and unification, originality, relation, and reciprocal adaptation? Have there always been being, existence, existents? Will there always be? Must we not admit, with the friend of the Time Traveler, that *"for me the future is still obscure and empty, a vast unknown . . ."*[93]

Perhaps it may be that prediction implies predetermination but that the contrary is not true, i.e., that the future is predetermined and we do not know this. When it is a question of us and our transitive activity transforming the world around us, and our immanent activity transforming ourselves, then the problem encompasses that of freedom, choice, and project. There are some who think that prediction can be determining without itself being determined.

Individual virtualities and realizations according to modern genetic theory. Predictions relative to the individual, the group, and the species.
The biological theory currently in favor is Mendelian, mutationist, Darwinian, and in profound opposition to the views of Lamarck. It maintains Darwin's position that biological evolution results from genetic variations at random in confrontation with the necessity of adapting as well as possible.[94] The theory perhaps wants for a little more prudence in its belief that it has resolved all difficulties, and in its use of facts as proofs when the same facts could as well be invoked in favor of another theory.

With increasing precision, we perceive the structure of the gene, the physico-chemical mechanism of its autoreproduction and variation and of the direction that it gives to the individual construction. We begin to see some pheno-genotypal retroactions, but it is claimed that these are simple functional regulations which are not suited to change the genome significantly in regard to the evolution of the species. The genome is looked upon as a real virtuality. But we generally do not know whether, given the fact that everything is equal in the environment, the virtuality is that of a development identical to that of the progenitor, or of an analogous development that allows, along with repetitions, differences admissible by the organism in relation, or of an hereditary bad seed more or less precociously lethal, of a congenital inferiority in the struggle for life. To put it in another way, in most cases one is not able to detect a genetic virtuality before a realization begins. The two reasons for this difficulty are recombinations of the parents' genetic factors and the eventual variation of these factors. There are exceptions, such as the early diagnosis of the genetic sex, or of certain hereditary diseases, through the examination of the external morphology of the fetal chromosomes. We are rapidly coming to the point where we will achieve direct knowledge of finer genetic structures. Sometimes we are able to evaluate the relative quantity of genetic mutations for a species, for one epoch and under given conditions. Some factors that increase it are known, such as different radiations. Although it is possible to increase the rate of mutations, it is still not possible to order them qualitatively. Gene grafts have been done. Such is the recent progress of the already established science of genetic combinations initiated by Mendel.

As long as a genetic structure cannot be identified before any growth, prediction will be limited to the following alternative: in the case of a pure genetic race that excludes all mixture and all redistribution of the genes of its progenitors, all else being equal among external circumstances and other possible factors, then the process will be identical or analogous to what it was in the preceding generation. Either that, or it simply will not develop. If there is no identity but only analogy, the margin of variability for the differences that could come about can be known in broad outline and can consequently give rise to certain predictions to the extent that we have penetrated the concrete reality and the logic of the system. Thus it is that differences will necessarily have to preserve originality, and internal and reciprocal adaptation. Without it the organism will be unable to live. Within this kind of prediction-set, which is extremely general, other more detailed predictions can be made. Certain among them achieve the detail and the degree of certitude of physical and chemical laws, as when we say that under defined conditions an atom of oxygen and two atoms of hydrogen yield a molecule of water.

These conjoint tendencies towards diversification and unification, differentiation and reciprocal adaptation, originality of the parts and awakening of consciousness of the whole within them, perhaps merely constitute different aspects of a single, like way of being common to all living organisms. It is perhaps the sign, condition, and the moving force of life and of evolution, whether individual, social, or specific. This biological law, at the center of Darwinism but not exclusively Darwinian, would be coessential with life, the deepest, the most general, and the most enduring of laws. It would be a common modality persisting, analogically if you will, through all differences, emergences, evolutions and revolutions, and at the same time would be their originator and give them characterization. A certain necessity would thus emerge, and our knowledge would become more complete, concrete and universal, and our predictions less uncertain.

But is it not possible to have, or to conceive of, biological developments that are at once enduring and profoundly different from their precedents? Take human consciousness. Does it not go beyond the elementary reciprocal adaptation, sufficing to guarantee a minimum presumption of survival for the individual, and persistence for the group and species? Are these not assured as well, if not better, by less evolved intelligences? Or, better yet, by automatic reaction devoid of all understanding, by the delegation of reason, by the alienation of some or of all in favor of some or of all? Certain facts could induce doubt or make us forget that it is precisely this supplement of consciousness that characterizes our species.[95]

Point of view of the part and point of view of the whole.
The part is indeed pregnant with different futures, amounting to a virtuality of contraries and differences. Contrary to the opinion of Aristotle, this virtuality is not the exclusive domain of rational powers, which he confused with human knowing and ability, especially with our own art of medicine. But the multiplicity of virtualities and possible effects depends upon internal and external factors. Depending on circumstances, two atoms of hydrogen and one of oxygen will or will not yield one molecule of water, an hydrangea will be rose or blue, and an infant will remain undeveloped, will be reduced to a cog in a machine, or will be transformed into a man.

So have we done anything except shift the problem from the part to the whole? Does the whole, and consequently the part in relation, contain no more than one unique virtuality? Is its development predetermined from the start in a univocal way, as the Megarians maintained? Would creative evolution be no more than a rigid process of unfolding, an epigenesis fixed once and for all? As for human liberty and the existential project, could they be other than the conscious grasp of the necessity inherent in the development of the universe,[96][97] perhaps of the confrontation between chance and necessity? Some courageous theologians, not wholly satisfied by the dogma of human predestination and the imagery of sufficient grace, pose questions about God himself. Is He free to create or not create? Could He have created a world different than ours? Could He cease to maintain ours in existence?

4   *Special Modalities of Thought, and Particularly of the Knowledge of Time and Mistakes about Time. Solitude and Relation*

Developmental studies suggest that our logical structures and, in a general way, our ability to know arise out of a confrontation within the whole of reality, and that these are a sign of belonging and community of origin.[98] This presumption is strengthened when we see how a weakening of relationship affects our grasp of identity, difference, change, simultaneity, interval of time, order of succession, and real causality, diminishing, perverting and filling them with error and inversely how mental illness separates us from the world.

Relationships between sensorial deprivation and certain normal or abnormal modalities of thought. Dreams. Isolation.

While we are in restful sleep, our senses are partially asleep and our movements are curtailed. In suppressing any comparison between our sensations and our phantasms, this sensorial deprivation doubtlessly contributes to the illusion of actual perception, which is the first law of dreaming. In its own turn, this illusion seems to intervene in other particularities of dream thinking. Along with the surface unity of the dream, there is a further effort to conserve a little of the unity of time, place, action, and something of the identity and difference, that we have learned through daily contact. But psychoanalysis at the same time indicates a certain reciprocal adaptability and shows that these diurnal remembrances, fragments, materials, chosen and condensed unconsciously though usually not at random, are in other respects quite disparate. In addition to condensation, or conjointly with it, we see transformations, displacements, substitutions, sublimations, symbolizations, analogies, that are often no less unconscious, no less rich in deep affective meaning. The principle of identity is sometimes twisted outrageously. We can view a dead person as alive, a woman as a lion or a bull, without any amazement. With all the calm in the world, transforming a remembrance into an illusion of actual perception, I once observed myself in a dream about twenty or thirty meters in front of myself, on a deserted beach in the evening, looking at the sea . . .

Dream consciousness does not exclude all explicit reference to the real past or to something that appeared earlier in the dream, nor does it exclude all prediction or design. The illusion of actual perception itself is not immobile, but it unfolds in accord with its proper tempo, like a play, yet the real epochs of the diurnal fragments are mixed. Some apparent inversions of time, order of succession, and cause and effect, are often no more than an expression of a difficulty in arriving at clear consciousness of an affect, or the impossibility of the latter initially appearing in a way other than analogically, symbolically, in substitution, or disguised. Dreaming in my native French, I was under attack by a horse. It was expelling gas at me and trying to cover me with dung, and I was defending myself in the same way by expelling gas at the horse. After doing so, while still asleep, I burst out laughing at the "pun" I had made, improperly substituting "contre-petterie" for "contrepoint." Visual consciousness had preceded that of the word which had provoked it; together they were a condensation, with multiple substitutions, of combat problems, of a particularly noisy concert, of a conversation about *counterpoint,* and some other events.

In somewhat the same fashion, an external stimulus may trigger a dream destined to explain it, but it may appear changed in the dream and not perceived correctly until the dreamer awakes. Along with other methods (those for example that are based upon the electroencephalogram and eye movements during dreams) this sometimes allows us to compare time within the dream with the time of the dream itself. Apparently, there are great differences between the illusory duration of dream events and the real duration of the dream itself. The first would generally seem greater than the latter, and this would be partly explained by an album effect, or that of a film or speed reading, with only certain key points being represented. Nevertheless, discordances such as those described by Maury are surprising. It is doubtful that such a great number of historical events, such long conversations, which culminated in beheading, could have been imagined during the brief interval separating the collapse of a bed canopy on the dreamer and the dreamer's awakening. This does not correspond to the psychophysiological tempo as we know it. For instance, for a given subject in an awakened state, interior motorkinesthetic speech takes place at about the same pace as the word spoken aloud, and we have no reason to suppose that it is otherwise in the case of dreaming. Perhaps Maury was in a particularly deep sleep and did not awaken immediately.[99][100][101]

The sleep of the senses appears to contribute to the particular mechanisms of dream thinking, leading to a certain error and absence of logic, to a certain failure in adaptation to the common laws of reality. Facts such as these, hallucinations, periods of delirium, and difficulties in grasping astronomic time may have been observed in experimental isolation as in cases of blindness and deafness. This is not to say that a certain isolation may not be quite favorable for thinking: it is not possible to do serious work in an atmosphere of turmoil and agitation; audio-visual information should be moderated, selected, elaborated upon, and thought out. For a moment the mathematician forgets about experimental applications and sense representations, and the man of the spirit makes a retreat. The old Platonic dialectic between the senses and the intelligence continues to be essential, and even dreams are not devoid of meaning. If sensorial deprivation can deeply modify thought, for the better or for the worse, the contrary seems no less true. Great concentration of thought can be the cause of inattention and distraction. Mental illnesses can lead to a diminution and a distortion of the relationship between us and things: psychotic incoherence, disadaptation, autism, momentary diminution of hearing during the audio-verbal automatisms of chronic hallucinatory psychosis, etc.[102] In this correlation between sensorial deprivation and other thought changes, it is not always easy to tell which is the primary factor. Whatever the order of succession might be, or the relation of cause and effect, this correlation is without doubt sometimes no more than a particular case of the impossibility that we encounter when we try to devote ourselves to two different activities at once.[103]

Epilepsy. Neurosis. Other causes of stagnation, weakening and distortion of relationship.

In temporal epileptic crises, or when electricity is applied to temporal regions of the cerebral cortex, it happens that consciousness is invaded by a "vivid," compulsory, coercive recollection, and at the same time the subject is more or less cut off from the rest of the present situation. From the description which Penfield gives of them,[104][105] it is still not certain that in these "experiential responses" the illusion of real perception is as total as in dreams, nor that external relations are as sharply curtailed. However that may be, the hallucination is quickly criticized and recognized as such, contrary to other kinds of hallucinations.

Epilepsy shows us several kinds of disturbances in estimating time. While in hallucinatory recollection it is the past which invades the present, in the *déjà vu* or *déjà vécu* illusion it is the present which is wrongly projected into the past. In palinopsy or palinaudy, a perception gives rise to a hallucinatory reproduction. The patient has the illusion of seeing the same person pass before him several times, or of hearing the same noise repeated again and again.[106] Penfield maintains that in the course of the "experiential responses" the events are remembered in the same order in which they formerly occured. He did no systematic comparison between time in the real past, that within hallucination, and that of the hallucination itself. This last does not appear to exceed the time of electrical stimulation. In at least one case Penfield observed a large disparity between time within an hallucinatory recollection and that of the hallucination (a house was being repeatedly built and demolished over a very long period of time), which is suggestive of Maury's dream; perhaps, alongside an album effect, other critical distortions intervened in the subjective impression of duration.

In neuroses, we have still another way in which the past invades the present, with a whole retinue of unconscious relationship breakdown, failure in adaptation and understanding, contradiction, absurdity, lack of logic, disease symptoms, and pains that are in a way not justified. Under the influence of an inadequate, pathogenic environment, and perhaps also under the influence of a particular reactivity, there occurs an early fixation in the way of perceiving the world and behaving within it. In each new situation, the subject unconsciously analyzes what it has in common with those situations in which his neurosis was originally formed, and it continues to react in a fashion that is identical or analogous. His repetitive and stereotyped behavior is the less adapted and the more unfortunate to the extent that circumstances are changed and have outdistanced the initial situations through the passage of astronomical time. Constantly projecting his past into the present, and seeing the present through the past and the past in the present, he is unable to follow reality in its changes and explore a given situation in all its dimensions; the project itself, the imagined future, can only perpetuate the outdated valuations, desires, and fears. His relations with his physician initially give rise to the habitual repetition, which is rightly called "transference." The conscious grasp of all the present symptoms and of the way in which they came to be, the change in the psychotherapeutic relationship, are tantamount to the cure. The arrested infant within the adult has grown up, and henceforth the past yields to the present and the future.

There are many other things that cause an arrested growth, a weakening and distortion of the relation between the whole and the part, between reality and the subject. These causes are more or less interior to the subject, or more or less exterior: drugs, food deficiencies, accidents, illnesses, old age, rigidity of tradition, all manner of taboos, *autos-da-fé* and witch hunts . . . The most serious affective and intellectual retardations can be provoked by hindrances to freedom of thought, whether direct or indirect, visible or disguised, clumsy or underhanded, by the insufficiency or inappropriateness of instruction, education, family or social milieu, or of the economic and political regime. Neuroses constitute only a small part of this group.[107]

Truth and falsehood in dreams. Back again to Cartesian realism and unrealism.

It is above all the illusion of actual perception which has led to the popular opinion that dreams are deceptive. In addition to a perfectionism perhaps approaching the obsessional, and to a certain confusion between what we should try to demonstrate and what we should not, the strength of this illusion seems to have strongly contributed to Descartes's idealism: how to be certain that at this moment I am not dreaming, under the fallacious and compelling influence of an evil genius, a Prince of Lies? Several years ago, I had a dream about a friend of mine, an imposing Church dignitary. He was discoursing with me about the theory of knowledge when he suddenly changed into a naked little man sitting on my knee, covered with hair and afflicted with hypospadias. It seemed to me that his purpose was to ask me through images, without words, whether the reality of what I thought I was seeing needed a demonstration. My answer was "no." Perhaps Descartes would have answered "yes," and would have believed that he had made that demonstration by repeating in the dream his waking theory: "we discover God in us, and God could not wish to deceive us."

If it is true that in a certain fashion dreams separate us from reality, they are also deeply realistic. They form a part of ourselves. For one who knows their laws, they help to explain the dreamer, the dreamer in the world, and the world within the dreamer. True or false, healthy or diseased, free or hindered, contemporary or from the past, the diurnal, waking rapport between us and our own selves, and between us and the whole of the real, undergoes an analogical transformation in the dream. The deprivation of the external senses, the preponderance of visual imagery, the illusion of actual perception, the poetic symbolization, add a touch of drama.

Analytical psychotherapy uses dreams to understand and bring the patient to understand how abnormal survivances from the past within him are limiting the present and the future. Sometimes our dreams do a better job of shedding light on ourselves, others, and the world, than do our day-time thoughts. The ancients believed in the revelatory and prophetic character of dreams. A chemist made or completed his discovery of the structure of benzene in a dream, and if it is true that a massacre of innocents was in preparation, Joseph did well to follow his nocturnal inspiration and flee into Egypt. At the beginning of the age of man, feeling within himself the force of reason and of other instincts, setting before himself the great problems of *praxis,* philosophy and faith, foreseeing universal mathematics and the powers of man, Descartes saw in a dream a *corpus poetarum*—which he interpreted immediately as the sum of human knowledge—and the words: *"quod vitae sectabor iter?"*, what way of life shall I follow? and *"est et non."* During the course of the same night, before dreaming about the development of knowledge, liberty of universality, and being and nothingness, Descartes dreamed about the freedom of choice. Echoing Baillet, Jacques Maritain remarks how its imagery amused the eighteenth century readers of the philosopher's biography (who were already somewhat psychoanalyists): a melon was offered between two successive enterings into a church, the first free, the second compulsory . . .[108]

It can happen that a dream will offer us a dramatic interior intimation of infinite virtualities, an aspiration from totality, toward totality, of which our actual limitations, the chains to break and the necessary refusals, are in a way the reverse; one must die to himself in order to live a true life, leave the port in order to sail the high seas. But concentration, symbolization, and dramatization aside, do these dreams teach us anything beyond what others have experienced during their waking hours? The St. Anselms, the Descartes, Hegels, Feuerbachs, Marxs, and Lenins, and doubtless millions and millions of parishioners from all parishes during all communions, perhaps every man as a sign of his humanity, and perhaps even some of our predecessors in the evolution of species?[109] May we not discern in the most humble living creature the roots, as it were, of this tendency towards universality? It is God who places it within us, or is it we who create God? If the story is true, as avowed, what did President Mao Tse-tung mean when he once claimed that he had seen God? Day or night, awake or asleep, the feeling of an infinitude within us, or a freedom from limitation, is in a sense enlightening. But this should be interpreted, or an attempt should be made to do so, in the light of all knowledge or of faith. The overturning of St.

Anselm's argument, so common among humanity, should move Christian philosophers and theologians towards greater prudence in their apologetic: Christian faith is founded not only upon such an aspiration within us, aided by the review of Mary and Joseph's dreams, but upon many other motives of credibility or incredibility. One could say the same about a good number of other beliefs.

Solitude, purgation, relation.

There is a certain amount of exterior tranquility, a certain isolation and withdrawal from involvement that favors meditation, the discernment of the essential, and the deepening of relationship. But the noise, the congestion and disorder, can be within us, and it is within us that it behooves us to establish silence and free our attention.

Descartes's method is that of intellectual purgation and scientific asceticism: *"to take nothing for true that does not seem to me either evident or demonstrated."* Psychoanalysis helps us to purge our affections as well as our intelligence, to remove the frills and to see. It is from an affective and intellectual purgation, from the silence of the night, that the light of the mystics may arise, even to the point of that mysterious utterance of Theresa of Avila which she is to have made at her death: *"Todo y nada."* However we might ask whether their great intuitions may not have been occasionally ahead of the rest of their science, their affective purgation in advance of their intellectual, and if the same interior experience may not be interpreted differently according to different ways of knowing and believing.

Between my twentieth and twenty-fifth year, I also experienced a kind of purgation. A propensity toward making contacts and to solitude, a long rigorous retreat full of hard work, friendships, conferences, conversations, reading, meditation and study at the *Sanatorium des Etudiants de France* and later at the *Swiss University Sanatorium,* the conflict within myself between complementary or contrary ideas, conflict initially felt passively and later actively sought after—all of these elements started a kind of interior scouring on my part. It seems to me that this has continued, through the vicissitudes of fortune, in relationship and reflection, in my practice of life, of medicine, and of psychanalysis, beginning with my own. It was doubtless not so much a matter of the true having so frequently replaced the false, but that the false certitudes had at least made room for the knowledge of my own ignorance, for a spirit of openness and research. With due reverence to proportions, this approach in its initial stages resembled that of Descartes. I had arrived at a certain degree of what I then called the experience of the void, when a deep anxiety seized me, which perhaps contributed to my use of psychological means for achieving tranquility, means that today I would be tempted to find a little hasty and premature. Perhaps no less anguished is the cry of one of our confreres fighting against the mass of scientific information.[110] An overabundance of expression can itself constitute an obstacle:

"Oui ce vain souffle que j'exclus
Jusqu' à la dernière limite . . ."

B Biological and Human Development

1   *Mathematical, Physico-Chemical and Biological Points of View Regarding the Development of Living Beings*

Heredity and variations. Molecular combinations.
Long before the recent progress of molecular biology, genetics had arrived at a certain number of conclusions. What follows are some of the more commonly accepted. The genetic code would function for the making of the individual in the same way as does the architect's plan for the construction of a house. It would be located in the chromosomes and not in the cytoplasm. Prior biological evolution would deliver the code fully prepared at the birth of each new living organism. Depending on the case, it would remain unchanged throughout the entire lifetime of the individual and its descendents, or it would change. It would therefore be endowed with a power of conservation, of memory and heredity, that is to say a power of auto-reproduction, and also a power of variation. Whatever may be its mechanisms, change of species is a fact. As paleontology begins to show us transitional forms, it assures us of the reality of a continuous evolution (which does not mean one without temporary accelerations), and the theory of successive deluges and the transformist-fixist views of Baron de Cuvier have but few defenders today.[111] The only living organisms that can subsist and perpetuate themselves are those which are sufficiently adapted.

First of all molecular biology evidences an encasing of combining agents within combining agents, a little like the alphabet is to words, words to phrases, and phrases to discourse . . . Simple substances such as carbon, oxygen, hydrogen, and nitrogen, have the mathematical possibility of an immense number of combinations. In the course of biological development they will be seen to yield four defined composite substances, the purine and pyrimidine bases. In their own turn the latter arrange themselves in various ways along the chains of desoxyribonucleic acids that make up chromosomes, and these new elements would have yielded as many different and enduring combinations as there are species and races. The combinations which have been realized and which have persisted were mathematically, chemically, and biologically possible. A still greater number would have been mathematically and chemically possible, and many among them realized in the course of evolution but not in an enduring fashion because they were biologically incapable of living.

Theories of evolution.

Molecular or premolecular, the majority of modern geneticists tend to link their teachings not to Lamarck but rather to Darwin and mutationism. The elementary variation would consist in a mutation, that is a sudden change within the molecule of desoxyribonucleic acid, one letter of the purine and pyrimidine alphabet being replaced by another. It would be fortuitous and happen by chance, yet in no way would it signify indetermination. It would be simply the result of an independent causal series. Depending on the moment at which the mutation occurred, it would or would not have an effect on the development of the individual undergoing the change and could or could not be transmitted to its decendents. From the start it would be hereditary and would be conserved by replication and autoreproduction as long as the changed organism and its decendents would survive and as long as no new change in the genetic molecule would happen at the same location. The changed individuals would not develop and perpetuate themselves unless the genetic changes were acceptable by the organism and its relationships, and unless the new characterization led to advantage in the competition for life. The internal factors of selection would predominate in respect to the mutations that were precociously lethal. The factors of environment and the struggle for life and for the perpetuation of the species would not intervene until after a certain level of individual development. The criterion of selection would be that which makes for the best reciprocal adaptation.

Though the proportion of mutants within a population is usually small, compared to the geological ladder of time and among the innumerable multitudes of living beings which the earth has known, the absolute number of effectively realized combinations in spatial sequences of purine and pyrimidine bases within the molecules of nucleic acids, though undoubtedly less than the mathematically possible combinations, must nevertheless have been literally enormous. That is at least what Darwin's theory postulates when it makes of chance variation a kind of matter or material cause for evolution, the marble that would ceaselessly be worked by the sculptor's chisel to give it form, i.e., the selection eliminating every combination that is biologically inadequate, or at least less adequate than others. The selection would therefore represent the final and formal causes of ancient philosophy, and at the same time the efficient cause that it holds in common with modern science. It is in this sense, as Jacques Monod has expressed it, that biological evolution would be the fruit of chance and necessity. It also would show the result of a conflict between environment and living creature, the two fluctuating between conservation and variation, of a contradiction that is not interior to the organism but rather to the whole that it consitutes along with its surroundings.

Beyond doubt the theory of Darwin represents a grandiose attempt to explain evolution and revolutions in the world of life. A very large number of facts seem to bear it out. It is not, however, without obscurities and difficulties, or at least not without problems that still remain unresolved. As large as has been the number of chance genetic variations, if we consider the innumerable innate behaviors geared to internal and external adaptation, would not the probability of the formation of the corresponding genetic combinations be nul or minimal? Would the struggle for life in the microenvironments whence stream the victors be sufficient to explain the general coexistence of organisms belonging to extremely different levels of evolution? If it proves to be correct that throughout the course of the evolution of species complex organs have been formed progressively, even though at the beginning they were unable to function and consequently were of no use for the initial members of these evolutionary lines, though not a hindrance for them, then how might this be reconciled with the Darwinian scheme of things?

Lamarckism might perhaps better resolve the first problem: in former times it was the vogue to think that the "marvels of instinct," observed among animals that were otherwise regarded as witless, were remembrances inherited from more intelligent ancestors, or at least the result of individual, successive learning experiences that had become hereditary. It seems to solve the second two problems no better than Darwinism. Further, Lamarckism offers two great difficulties. It would never be observed that characteristics which parents acquired through practice and learning might be genetically transmitted to offspring. How the learned corporeal and mental modifications might come to be inscribed in the germinal cells of the testicle or ovary would escape comprehension. Molecular biology is becoming aware of somatogerminal relations other than these indirect ones of Darwinian selection: for example when the organism is undergoing moments of development and operation and the effectuating genes are being activated or inhibited through cytoplasmic influences, which can be a function of exterior changes.[112] But even though it can appear surprising that action or inaction, and the fact of entering or not entering into unstable chemical combinations, may have no deeper effect on them, it would remain unconfirmed that changes in the structural genes under the influence of these centripetal activating or inhibiting relations are other than functional and momentary.[113] Cerebral biochemistry, however, is beginning to speculate whether the mnemonic traces that are formed during the course of individual development might not resemble genetic molecules, and even if they might not be transported from the neurons to the adjoining neuroglia and there placed in reserve. The transference of experience from one hemisphere to the other appears to be better demonstrated.[114]

Genetic and environmental influences on individual development.
There is thought to be a strict correspondence between the spatial distribution of the score of amino-acids constituting the body's proteins and that of the four purine and pyrimidine bases of the genetic code. With this process of translation molecular biology can begin to glimpse the mechanism involved in the construction of the individual, and how this individual is a function of the architectural plan assigned to it at birth. It certainly does not forget that the organism is equally a function of its environment. With the discovery of sulfamides, one of the glories of the new Pastorian school is the discovery that operational and structural genes are regulated extragenetically by exterior and interior environments, through the intermediary of repressive genes.[115] However, perhaps due to a microscope effect that hinders viewing the whole (a little like the trees that hide the forest from us, and the forest the countryside), molecular biology sometimes seems to assign more weight to centrifugal action, that which arises from the genetic plan and moves outward towards the formation of the periphery. The word "epigenesis" occasionally seems to be taken in the sense of a univocal explicitation of genetic virtualities, or at least in the sense of the relatively narrow margin of the phenotypal changes that are a function of the environment.

It seems to be admitted that the primary conformation of proteins is linear, defined by the order of succession of their amino-acids, and that this order is exclusively a function of that of the purine and pyrimidine bases in the genetic molecules. The proteins would then take on a secondary pseudo-globular conformation. This would contain new possibilities of combinations grafted on to the preceding ones, because each protein, from the purely mathematical point of view, could take a considerable number of different globular forms. These new possibilities would find themselves practically annulled and univocal genetic determination restored by the fact that, for one defined linear sequence, only one globular form would be stable and enduring. This restriction, however, would hold true only if the environment remains unchanged. Finally, the geometric structure of the globular protein, and as a consequence the nature and spatial distribution of its free and active chemical groupings and its functional modalities, are considered as a function at once of the genetic code and of the environment, and are thus subsumed under the general biological law.[116]

The psychophysiological level. Combinations of neurones.
We must now consider another problematic, another level of evolution: our highest activity, whose introspective aspect we call the mental life. Experience teaches us that we are able to understand the universe. In a sense, so to speak, we are able to contain it. Though this aptitude is indeed bestowed on us by heredity, its realizations are not, for all that, inscribed in us from the start; they express the relations that we establish as individuals, even though filtered through the body social and civilization. To what does this correspond from the neurophysiological viewpoint? Ramon y Cajal has taught us that the elementary neural unity is the neurone, i.e., the nerve cell. In the human fetus a part of the embryonic neurones would disappear in the course of the final weeks of pregnancy.[117] Despite this, their number and the number of neurones derived from them is enormous. Their number does not increase with time, but until adulthood each neurone continues its arborization, that is its connections with other neurones.[118] [119] The number of possible routes for neural activity increases in quasi-geometric proportion. This immense network of outer and inner connections sees its possibilities increase still more by the fact that not only are the anatomical routes of significance, but even more so their functional modalities. These are described actually in spatial and temporal terms of summations of elemental excitations and inhibitions, which give rise to unitary neuronic discharges.[120] [121] In addition to this, there are some still uncertain glimmers

about possible molecular mechanisms for recording remembrances. The number of possible combinations, as say the mathematicians, tends towards infinity: such seems to be the anatomophysiological and corporeal aspect of our power to understand the world, to understand ourselves, and to act in compliance with this knowledge.[122]

The successive encasing of combining agents within combining agents contributes to characterize the degrees of development, conservation and emergence, the transformation from quantity to quality, the breaks, leaps, stages, levels, and revolutions within evolution. This coincidence between the most classic form of dialectic and the most up-to-date data of the natural sciences is not surprising. Just as the ancient atomists had extrapolated in the analytical direction what they could observe about the divisibility of bodies, so did classical dialectic extrapolate in the synthetic way that which the science of the times had observed exactly: two atoms of hydrogen and one atom of oxygen yield one molecule of water, and when liquid water is heated to one hundred degrees centigrade it is suddenly tranformed into vapor . . . Even then, every effort must be made so that the dialectic of thought corresponds to the dialectic of the real in general, that of the part to that of the whole. At every level of evolution under study, our analyses and syntheses should as much as possible be grounded in reality, be concrete, and be exhaustive. As for the fact that in this upward thrust of evolution and revolutions we seem to see more arise from less, this should in no way disturb the believers. Indeed, in their opinion or in the opinion of certain among them has not God, who is the All, immanent or transcendent, created the world *ex nihilo?* Or, if we admit that these words be meaningful, does He not create Himself?

The driving and emotional aspects of the subject in relation are called "affectivity," from *afficio,* to tend towards, and *affecto,* to affect, to move. Every drive is not necessarily conscious. Every emotion is conscious. All consciousness in a certain way involves both drives and emotions. A drive can be at once unconscious and logical, when characterizing the unconscious relationships of reciprocal adaptation, relations that are in a sense truthful, veracious, or true. Inversely, a drive can be at once illogical, ill-adapted, erroneous, and conscious, or at least can be accompanied by an obscure consciousness. Reason, or logic that is conscious and endowed with a certain universality, is fundamentally related: it assists in the satisfaction and control of the other affects, while at the same time being profoundly affective in itself. Without the perspective of affectivity there is not much that we would understand about human development: in relation to the whole of the real, to the other, the others and himself, man in the world is moved and affected—*"mu et ému."* Drives are observable from outside among other beings and, one could say, this extends to the physico-chemical world. We make analogical and hypothetical inferences, with more or less semblance to truth, from our own emotions and from our conscious motivations in general, to those of other living beings who, in other respects, especially in their behavior and their nerve coordination, are more or less similar to us.

Differentiation and unification. Conservation and emergence.
Arising out of relations within the totality and continuing to participate in them, living organisms both persist and change at the same time. They reproduce and they evolve, among differences and emergences conserving characteristics common to the rest of reality, to the physical world, and to themselves, doing so within increasingly restricted and particularized biological groups down to concrete individuals. These common domains

indicate community of origin, and they are the sign and the condition of the relation. The relation as much as the originality is the essential feature of the living being. Perhaps the originality is explained by the relation. For Darwin the advantage that is associated with the greatest reciprocal adaptation would be the moving force of evolution. For him, without any paradox, far from resulting in coincidence and uniformity, it would be the cause, the *"raison d'être"* of biological differentiation and, at the same time, of reality's dawning awareness of itself among animals and men, that is to say a higher form of unification. In the dominant genetic theory, which is Mendelian, mutationist, and Darwinian, the hereditary patrimony bestowed upon each individual by preceding generations would be expressed in the phenotype either univocally or variably according to circumstances, which means within the relation. The phenotype in relation would be the touchstone by which the whole would judge the mutation to be either worthy or unworthy of enduring, and it would be this judgment that would promote the evolution of species. The internal correlations are no less important.

Reciprocal adaptation is apparent everywhere. The individual and the group adapt themselves to the exterior environment and transform it. The individual adapts itself to the group at the same time that it helps to create the group and adapts the group to it. Each of us needs material, spiritual, social, civilizing sustenance; but without us the group, society, civilization, and species would die out.

Homeostasis or constancy of the interior environment helps to characterize the preservation of originality and individuality, conservation, restoration and growth according to a defined type. It is linked to alimentation, digestion, assimilation or rejection, elimination, and cellular functions in general. It defines the limits within which certain physico-chemical characteristics of the organism can change without danger, at least under normal conditions. Lack of nourishment, water, or air, diminishes the concentration of blood sugar or increases that of mineral salts or carbonic acid. Directly or through the intermediary of inner senses, regulating nerve centers are activated. Interior changes take place, such as the freeing of reserves, reduction of use and losses. At the same time one experiences hunger, thirst, the need to breathe, and one seeks alleviation, appeasement, satisfaction, well-being, and satiety. This quest often demands a lot of work, learning, and ingenuity.

Relation, pleasure, displeasure, biological logic that links displeasure to danger, pleasure to utility for the individual, group or species, innate behaviors, learned behaviors, conditioned reflexes and the rational quest for satisfaction: already some broad articulations of the dialectic of affectivity are visible in these elementary biological functions as they serve to maintain the constancy of the interior environment, yet remaining the conditions and beginning of change, and particularly of that change which, for living organisms, consists in the ever increasing understanding of the universe to which they belong.

Psychoanalytical point of view.

Psychoanalysis did not wait for progression in psychophysiology and comparative physiology of behavior to elaborate a theory of drives and emotions. In the preceding examples concerning homeostasis and its momentary rupture Freud would have referred to the "internal origin" of the process; he would have called the internal sense receptors and the nerve centers stimulated by the change of interior environment "sources of tension;" the air, the drink and the food would have been "objects;" the lungs and the digestive apparatus, "ways of achieving satisfaction;" and the "goal," "objective" "aim" or "purpose," perhaps better called consequence or effect, would have been the reestablishment of homeostasis and the appeasement of hunger, of thirst, or of the need for air. There are many internal origins. The sources of excitation and tension are as numerous as the sense and nerve receptors. In hunger and thirst, the dryness of the mouth and the emptiness of the stomach no doubt constitute only some factors among others. The exterior objects able to appease by reestablishing equilibrium should contain some defined chemical bodies: oxygen, water, proteins, fats, carbohydrates, vitamins, minerals, etc. . . . But some large variations are allowed outside this common condition. When necessary, hunger and thirst—though not of the gourmet—can be momentarily satisfied in ways other than oral. The infant's breathing is initially taken care of by the placenta. Biological utility is most often unconscious, and it is sometimes neglected in favor of harmful pleasures. *"Ersatz,"* drugs, alcohol, can be preferred to genuine nourishment. Mice have been known to give themselves over to the pleasures of electric autostimulation and die of starvation. The latter can be done for more noble reasons, apparently without suffering too much; as for thirst, it appears to involve more intense sufferings. More prosaically, Minvitine Wander and Pondinil Sauter help the obese person reduce by deceiving the periphery and the centers. Thus while still on the subject of the major common biological behaviors, eating, drinking, and breathing, we begin to catch sight of the complexity involved in what Freud spoke of as the destiny of the drives.

As progress in the study of affectivity goes on, we catch further glimpses of the multiplicity of internal origins, the diversity and variability of the organs capable of being excited, the paths towards satisfaction, the objects affording satifaction, the relationships between pleasure and other uses, between univocal genetic explicitations and more flexible conditioning, learning and reasoning behaviors, between the individual and the group, between, as the psychoanalysts say, the *"id,"* the *"super-ego,"* and the *"ego."* The internal origin is often less well known than in the case of hunger, thirst, and the need to breathe. Sexuality, which was especially studied at the beginnings of psychoanalysis, manifests hormonal variations according to chromosomal sex, age, cycle, maternity, etc., and above all an extraordinary variety of behaviors, objects, and organs related to excitation, even though they do not lead to complete satisfaction. This latter is not limited to orgasm, but involves a whole gamut of different emotions as well: those, for example, that parents and infants can experience in their mutual relations. Often the excitation is sought for its own sake, and the orgasmic satisfaction is delayed or excluded. Sexuality further manifests a noticeable tendency towards disassociation between what are sometimes called the goals of the individual and those of the group or species, in other words between different pleasures, uses and consequences. The drives and the emotions characterize the transitive relationships we have with the outside world, or those that are immanent and inward directed, as in the case of narcisism. They characterize relations with full and actual concrete reality, or with phantoms, phantasms, recollections, projects, anticipations, or dreams; or it may be preferable to say that the imagination itself is pro-foundly affective, whether it be chimerical, reproductive, anticipatory, or creative. It would also be possible that drives and emotions can take place without any object.[123] Opposed or simply different affective tendencies conflict or come to terms with each other. Repressions, defenses, com-promises, displacements, substitutions, sublimations and other transforma-tions take place.[124]

Ethological point of view.
Perhaps even more than psychology, classical physiology, psychoanalysis, and even genetic epistemology, but along with them and in relationships of mutual support with them, ethology or comparative physiology of behavior, Pavlovian reflexology, and ontogenetic psychophysiology have begun to

show us the relations between heredity and individual and social learning. In modern genetic theory it would doubtless be better to speak of degrees of the genotype's permissiveness in regard to phenotypal realizations and behaviors, and of degrees of the phenotype's independence in regard to a genotype taken as chemically defined.

Within behaviors called instinctual or innate, in the sense of being strictly and rigidly preadapted by prior biological evolution, with a very weak margin for individual adaptability, the internal pole is a stereotyped functional automatism, which is always the same; the external pole is a triggering sign. Under ordinary conditions, those which saw these kinds of behaviors materialize in the course of the evolution of species, these triggering signs are contained in the objects or situations able to mobilize the automatism in a way that may, at the same time, be satisfying for the individual and otherwise useful for it, the group, and the species. Satisfaction aside, utility is generally completely unconscious, as when an insect lays its eggs on a paralyzed caterpillar and, in so doing, stores fresh food for the offspring it will never see, whose future existence it cannot even suspect; nevertheless the relation is fundamentally one of reciprocal adaptation and mutual convenience, and in this sense that relation is logical and true. But the slightest disturbance brought to bear on exterior conditions shows up the animal's lack of intelligence, its slavery to a sign, its inability to understand the whole. The triggering sign, even though it is generally built on the principle of the lock and key so as to reduce the risk of reaction in inappropriate situations, is nevertheless common to circumstances that are more or less different in other respects, that is, analogous; this already makes for some softening of the univocity and rigidity of innate behaviors.[125]

Two functions of intelligence. The tendency towards universality. Limitations.

Even among species that are relatively little evolved we observe an individual aptitude to seek out situations that contain the innate, triggering sign, and are able to set in motion the automatic sequence and thereby make for satisfaction. These behaviors of seeking and orientation, tropisms or others, are particularly visible among living organisms that are endowed with mobility; but the least selectivity of a nutritive substance, the least selective permeability of a membrane, represent basically processes of the same order. As the progress of the species goes on, these take on ever greater importance and contain increasing amounts of conditioning, learning, consciousness, reason, and of the capacity to understand the whole. This aptitude towards seeking is also very clearly innate, but it is so precisely as an aptitude, a virtuality. If not from that of the whole, from the viewpoint of the individual, of the part, the explicitations and realizations are neither obligatory nor univocal: they are dependent upon exterior circumstances as well as upon genetic virtualities.

The seeking behaviors are initially at the service of the other drives and instinctual satisfactions, of the other uses. But without thereby losing these primordial functions they tend to separate themselves partially from them, developing themselves, in a way, for their own sakes, and emerging as no less powerfully instinctual, emotional and affective than the others, with the most profound pleasures of their own. It is possible to reward a rat for its successes in a problem box by offering new objects for its curiosity. The child explores, examines, questions. The mathematician, Pavlov used to say, is directed towards the truth as the plant towards light. Beyond a certain level of evolution the microcosm bears within itself the possibility of understanding the universe, and it tends towards the realization of this virtuality with all its forces. This tendency towards unification without coincidence, through the grasp of consciousness, is complementary to the tendency towards the conservation of differences, one modality of which is the homeostasis of the interior environment. It is not exempt from conservation and memory. It is not reducible to the inconsistent waverings of temporary liaisons at the whim of local changes and tides.

An evolved form of seeking conduct, intelligence remains partially at the service of the other drives. These can be educated, they can yield to controls, defenses, repressions, substitutions, displacements, and sublimations, to psychosomatic conversions and to various other transformations; but in a general way these transformations bear on relations rather than on internal origins. At the present state of our knowledge these internal origins are often resistant to modification: it is necessary to breathe, drink, and eat; certain functionings can be modified deeply, but it is preferable to avoid the example of Origen: he found his sexuality scandalous, God knows why, and we all know the way in which he cut short the question; bromide is no better. Be that as it may, there we have one source of limitations.

Even in modalities that are the most removed from primordial instincts, and even if we are virtually able to understand the world, other limitations intervene: the brevity of our life, social conditions fostering ignorance, and all manner of obstacles to encounters, relations, and to the deepening of these relations. And but think, as did Pascal, of the dimensions of the universe, of the number of stars, of atoms . . .

The confrontation between the living organism and its surroundings can itself have a reducing and limiting effect; realizations resulting from some encounters can hinder other realizations. If conditioned reflexes, the "temporary linkages," are fundamentally reversible, it is not so in the case of other modalities of memory, learning, and habits. These last mentioned, whether good or bad, are often tenacious, especially when they were formed in infancy: it is as if an impression was made in soft wax which then hardened. The young swan who saw Lorenz at birth took him for his mother definitively. The neurotic fails to perceive anything in the present or future except the past. If the laborer or the specialized worker has been too poorly or too badly formed he quickly becomes too dated to be "recycled," as they say. To the extent that we make progress in life, make choices for ourselves, or see life make choices for us, doors close that doubtless were open for us at another time. More generally, our past is what it is; it has definitely escaped from change, and to it the memory makes reference.[126] The latter, however, constitutes a factor of development as well; conservation, one of the conditions of emergence.

Another source of limitations is found in the tendency to delegate reason, to blind obedience. This tendency is observable in a number of social species, our own included. It is opposed to the individual's exercise of his own intelligence. Unreasoning submission and intelligent activity can consolidate in different fashions in the division of labor, the military defense of the group, etc. . . . Both, in combination with the biological logic of innate behaviors, can contribute to the greatest rationality of the whole, of each and of all, or of certain privileged individuals in this regard.

As for the so-called phenomenological limitation, which Kant believed necessary to attribute to our knowledge, complaining that the latter does not coincide with reality, and separating us from reality by the twofold opaque screen of the senses and the intelligence, we have shown that it is illusory.

Return to Freud and psychoanalysis. Truth and insufficiencies in the "second topic."

Following the distinction between what is conscious and what is not, retrieving and making it more precise without abolishing it, Freud's "second topic" describes three "places" or "regions of the psyche." The coincidence with the data of other biological and human sciences is not complete, but the differences are as enlightening for them as for psychoanalysis.

The "id" is the place of drives, of emotions, of pleasures and displeasures that are in a certain way elementary. They are minimally conscious, and as soon as the reasonable "ego" or the "super-ego" enters the picture, these latter exhibit a nuance of surprise, incredulity, indignation, fear, defense, refusal . . . "that does not interest me" . . . "that is not true," etc. . . . Freud in no way reduces the behaviors of the id to innate instinctual manifestations stripped of learning: already in the id a certain education of the drives and emotions is evident, whether for good or for ill. The "super-ego" is the totality of the demands of society and family, which are unconsciously introjected rather than examined in a rational way and consequently accepted.[127] The "ego" is the conscious or unconscious organ of adaptation of the id's drives and emotions to the exterior world, and particularly to social demands. It is also what is most conscious and reasonable within us.[128] [129]

It is not certain that Freud perceived the existence of innate instinctual behaviors other than oral, combative, and sexual. But who can affirm that the spirit of service (other than the case of mutual support between husband and wife, and caring for the needs of children, often quite colored by sexuality) is an acquired trait in the case of man? And what of the penchant towards hierarchy, territory, and property—be it only the need for a certain guarantee of personal independence? If all these are so visibly innate in other species, why should they have been completely transformed in our own species into the fruit of learning, of civilization, of the unconscious introjection of the injunctions of the group, or of personal reasoning?

Further, innate behaviors such as those observed in other species and even in our own, especially toward the beginning of life, are doubtless colored by no more than an elementary consciousness; but under normal conditions they are remarkably adapted: before any reason, they are the very condition for the continuation of life. The same can be said as well of the drives and emotions of the id, be they innate or learned: they have no need for the ego to be in a certain way already related and logical.

Finally, no more than the intelligence which serves to charaterize it, is the ego reducible to the quest for satisfactions other than those which accompany its own proper activity, or to the calculus of pleasure and pain, or to the quiet and unreasoned introjections of the group's injunctions. This last function has been more wisely referred to the super-ego. The reason in relation, without foresaking its other biological use, tends to develop itself for its own sake. Man finds great satisfaction in his increasing understanding of the world and himself. But with what could be called the generalized principle of pleasure, Freud had already gone beyond the first approximations of the "second topic" and was beginning to rejoin some other classic philosophies of happiness.

Affective object. Analysis and synthesis grounded in reality.
Knowledge of the other. Conjoint variation.

We can speak of affective objects in the same way as we have spoken of the objects of the senses, of the intelligence, etc.; they are all closely bound together. The object properly belongs to neither of the two terms of the relationship. It constitutes a primary analytic modality of the relationship, not unlike a surgical field. It does not exclude synthesis. Analysis and synthesis are both grounded in reality to some extent.

This is the double analytic and synthetic characteristic of the object, grounded in reality, that Spitz describes when the infant synthesizes aspects of the mother that were initially dissociated.[130] We can see a similar process in the evolution of species when individual knowledge of one's social partner succeeds triggering signs outside of context.[131] Once we become adults we understand that the person is at once an original being and a network of relations. Here again, too great an attachment to the part, whether innate or learned, can hinder understanding of the whole, the reunification in the mind of that which is really united outside of the mind but initially separated by the mind. Synthesis can succeed in a certain way and miss the mark in another. We know the difficulties we have in distinguishing the person beneath the sign and not reacting blindly and undividedly to it, while on the other hand, in another way, the unity of the person is recognized and can even have been the object of a theoretical elaboration: a partition of the other and of ourselves which can offer advantages and drawbacks.[132]

Sometimes the affective relationship contains so much reciprocal action that we are dealing with a true conjoint variation: such is the case of the evolution of the "dyad" composed of mother and child. In the psychoanalytic relation, the physician understands the patient and assists him in achieving self-understanding, in changing and being cured; in so doing the physician changes his object; the action is not in one direction only: without even mentioning countertransference, the experience of the psychotherapist increases. In a general way, when something is placed in relation it either modifies the other, i.e., the first term of the relationship, or not, and in different degrees; for example, there is a great difference between the discrete observation of a wild animal in its natural habitat and its observation in captivity, experimentation, dissection, etc. . . . This question has already been examined in regard to the theory of knowledge; the first term was defined as the reality that is independent of the fact of being knowable and which is not necessarily modified by the fact of being known. When it is modified, its reconstruction by thought remains possible, its past at any rate is known, and the temporal interval between its past and the present knowledge of it by another being has minimal theoretical impact: a considerably greater time difference, due to the fact that the propagation of light is not instantaneous, has never troubled astrophysicists. But the overriding point is that the conjoint variation characterizes relations of reciprocal adaptation and especially man "in situation," man acted upon and acting, knowing and transforming the world, knowing and transforming himself.

In what do pleasure and happiness consist, or, to put it better, the different kinds of pleasure and happiness? As interior states they are *sui generis*, indefinable, a little like certain principles of knowledge. We can scarcely presume that within other beings they resemble our own the more these beings resemble us in other ways: it is in grounding ourselves on the analogy of other aspects that we presume an analogy of interior states among "those more or less like ourselves," i.e., other men and our lesser brothers, the animals. But it is not impossible to approach these interior states, whether experienced or inferred, in another way, to describe the circumstances of their appearance, their anatomophysiological concomitants, evolution, and meaning; in a word, to make of them a natural history and philosophy, even a moral philosophy . . .

There are some observations and analogical hypotheses that are commonly accepted. Above all, the individual seeks to satisfy himself. Satisfaction is initially linked to the unfolding of innate, reactional programs, delivered complete by evolution and not requiring any learning. Depending on the species of animal, innate behaviors can result in different transformations at contact with the external environment, but these transformations have more of a bearing on the manner of establishing the relation than on the internal pole of the behavior. Despite the possible existence of reactions without any object, suggested by Lorenz, satisfaction is normally obtained in relation. As a certain progress takes place among species and individuals, primitive needs are better put into relation, and the quest for situations geared toward their satisfaction grows in perfection. At the same time intelligence starts to disengage in part from these primitive functions, and what a French geologist called "the joy of knowing" arises and develops.[133] Regardless of whether these are or are not properly rational, the realization of our instinctual tendencies usually involves other benefits for the individual, group or species, in addition to satisfaction. Dissociations, however, have been observed.

From ancient times, naturalists, moralists, and philosophers have generally agreed that every living being endowed with consciousness seeks happiness. Only in appearance does the cold formalism of Kant and his categorical imperative escape the rule. The masochist himself delights in suffering.[134] Pleasure and happiness have been linked with change and the absence of change, with movement and immobility, with time and eternity; they have been associated with the senses and intelligence, in so far as the latter are considered knowing respectively what changes and what does not change; they have been related to matter, in the sense of atoms or virtualities, and to form or act, these latter being frequently thought to proceed from the Eternal Ideas, from the First Unmoved Mover, from God, or at least from a certain concept of God; they have been linked with body and soul, with the flesh and the spirit . . .[135]

Happiness tied to change and the absence of change, to differentiation and unification, to relation, awareness, peace and struggle.

In cases of hunger, thirst, and the need to breathe, homeostasis constitutes the internal origin, the power of the impulse towards objects able to assure the constancy of the interior environment. "Relaxation of tension," "return to equilibrium," "principle of Nirvana," "ataraxy," "eutumin": from Epicurus to Freud, what is here being expressed is doubtless the biological principle of immobility, of return to the previous state, the pleasure of not changing and the displeasure involved in changing, which accompany permanence, repetition, and the use of means to assure these. But there are already other ways of being, other emotions which manifest themselves in connection with these great functions in which dominate conservation, reparation, assimilation, and growth in accordance with an internal, genetically defined type. Aperitifs, culinary refinements, to say nothing of the *"trou normand,"* of the *vomitorium* of the wealthy Romans, and of the price of clean air (and silence) in the age of the internal combustion engine, all these show quite clearly that pleasure is not simply in relation to the reestablishment, and by whatever means, of the previous state.[136] Sexual excitement is pleasureable independently of the tranquility following orgasm, and in a manner distinctly different from it. Man, as the saying goes, clings to the good times. The ancient Chinese, an extremely refined people, systematically practiced the *coitus retensus*. Stimulation of all kinds are multiplied, right down to hormonal treatments. The charm of femininity and virility are sublimated in a thousand ways.

But there is more. Why would pleasure accompany only one part of our activities, those which consist in resisting change or in returning to the past, while we are developing, i.e., while we are at once changing and not changing? While the change within us involves efforts and conflicts, to the point of "dying to oneself," in order to rediscover oneself at a higher level of relation, truth, logic, consciousness, and universality? Work, struggle, aggression, sadism, war *"fraîche et joyeuse,"* [137] [138] [139] interior combat, growth in body and spirit, in power, knowledge, possession, all involve their own proper pleasures. The pleasure of research is not based only upon the hope of satisfying other needs in the object's relationship, but it consists as well in the exercise itself of reason in relationship as it grows in knowledge of the universe and effectiveness over it, and in knowledge of itself as knowing and effecting. Some among us believe they can add that eternal beatitude is the crown of happiness in flux and consists in the vision of God face to face. [140] [141] [142] [143]

The Stoics.

Man changes, and that change is the result of combat. We must constantly struggle against letting ourselves be trapped by what is partial in order to remain free in respect to the whole. Long before St. Francis de Sales, [144] the Stoics knew that it was necessary to renounce oneself and the world in order to gain the world and oneself. The abandonment of a certain reality or object, or rather of a certain blinding, limiting, enslaving relational modality, is more than compensated for by the happiness linked to the free exercise of reason in relationship with the whole of reality. At least in the sense of a tendency, a movement, an infinite perfectibility measured by reality beyond number, by our infinity and our imperfection, we have the feeling of being able to understand all and love all, if not to do all. For the Stoics, to follow reason obliged one to forsake other pleasures, but *"to follow reason is to follow all of nature,"* because human reason is a part, a summary, a commentary, a mirror of nature. Like the followers of Heraclitus, the Stoics made man part and parcel of nature, and made of nature a contradiction that begets movement. Just as much as Parmenides, Socrates, Plato, and Aristotle, who would so powerfully prepare for and reinforce Christian faith, philosophy, practice, and mysticism, they made of the "overriding indifference towards partial goods" the condition, sign, and corrolary of accession to freer and more universal relational modalities, and of that liberty of universality the source of genuine happiness. [145] But, at least at first sight, the *Weltanschauungen,* the conceptions of the world and of ourselves, and the eschatologies are quite different; is there achievement of the person in a motionless, eternal, transcendent, indwelling, all-absorbing God from which it receives existence and towards whom it tends, or is there dissolution in the great All, motionless or moving, or both at the same time and perpetually growing? It is in these perspectives that are located in turn Hegel, Feuerbach, Marx and the atheism of today that is so close to pantheism, while at the same time ring out the mysterious words of the dying St. Theresa of Avila: *todo y nada. . .*

Thus, human happiness is fundamentally linked to the exercise of reason, to the comprehension, the understanding of reality. It does not exclude other pleasures, but often demands a choice and this choice takes place through a struggle. One wonders if the moralists of effort, of interior struggle, consider these only as a precondition of happiness linked to the liberty of universality, or if they would allow them their own pleasures beside. Let us leave the question to the historians of philosophy.

The Epicureans.

All advocates of movement, Heracliteans like the Stoics, the Cyrenaics and the Epicureans were atomists as well, like Democritus. By means of an inspired extrapolation from the divisibility of bodies and the mobility of the fragments, they heralded modern physical science. Their soul was breath-like and consisted of particularly fluid and mobile atoms, and thus they foreshadowed what was to become the nerve impulse and the anatomophysiological aspect of the freedom of universality. They were at the same time skirting the trap of an atomic monism, of a mechanical, levelling materialism that denies novelty and aspects: this would lead to the absurdity of Cabanis's remark that he had never found a soul beneath his scalpel. They had a unitary view of man and for that reason they tended to deploy "all pleasures under one and the same genus," as the ancient philosophers said. One small disagreement existed: Epicurius thought that happiness consists in setting our atoms at rest, while Aristipus, perhaps more in keeping with the generality of atomic and Heraclitean views, thought that happiness consists in a movement, albeit a gentle one.[146]

Dualists.

Attenuated, if not actually suppressed by substantial union, the old dualism of soul and body frequently carries with it a corresponding division of pleasures. Given that the intellectual, separable soul dispenses with corporeal concomitants (except for a kind of matter, elements, virtualities, furnished by the senses, which on their part allow for corporeal concomitants and even demand them) the notion of pleasure is affected: there follows a tendency to separate sensible, carnal, perishable pleasures from the happiness of the soul, intellectual happiness, that happiness which is incorruptible and destined to survive beyond the pleasures of the body. From there to declare that there is opposition between the two orders of satisfactions involves but a small step, which we still see Bossuet take from the very first lines of his sermon on concupiscence. One further nuance: the senses would just reveal change; only the intelligence would touch upon eternal truths.

Kant.

The theory of the categorical imperative highlights both the illuminating and paradoxical character of Kant's doctrine. It artificially separates the "form of reason," that is its structure, mechanisms, laws, proper modalities (the principle of noncontradiction in the sense of formal logic) from the grasp that reason has of itself and from its exercise in relation with what is other than reason. In a kind of exception demanded by the system, reason sees its proper rule without the least phenomenal or categorial obfuscation arising from the senses and the intelligence, and it is there like an exceptional noumenal coincidence. The rule of reason must be respected because it is coessential with reason and to take no notice of it is equivalent to destroying reason. Pure reason at the same time is practical because, under pain of self-annihilation, it demands internal coherence regarding choice and the hierarchization of what we would now call "object relations." It is through these latter, by grasping the object, that we attain satisfaction, pleasure, and happiness. But happiness linked to the grasp of the object is phenomenal in a twofold sense: first, because all reality (save for the rule of reason) is initially grasped by the senses: *nihil in intellectu quod prior non fuerit in sensu;* second, because happiness linked to the grasp of an object constitutes an interior state that is apprehended by the intermediary of the internal senses, which are no less opaque than the others. It can be increased by a "self-satisfaction" linked to the fact that the rule of reason was respected.[147]

For the moment we will say nothing about the Cynics, the Skeptics, and those who know that they do not know a great deal but who continue to seek.

An abridgement of natural history and philosophy of happiness.
Quite briefly, what do we know, what can we presuppose about amusement, pleasure and happiness, without the risk of too much imprudence?

They are interior, mental, and introspective states which I experience and whose existence I presume, more or less hypothetically, without anthropomorphism and unconscious projection of subjectivity, in a more or less similar mode among a certain number of other living beings—animals, men, women, children—who more or less resemble me in other aspects, such as in their behavior and nervous system. Plants are of much more remote parentage. Pleasant or unpleasant, the emotions constitute a qualitative change in the universe, an emergence, a novelty. They accompany homeostasis, conservation, change, growth, peace, combat, impulses towards objects, the transitive or immanent relation of the organism with what is other than itself and with itself. The pleasantness often, but not always, fits in with other advantages for the individual, the group, or the species. In the first case, in addition to its own proper value, pleasure constitutes a supplementary regulation, a progression in reciprocal adaptation. In the contrary case it could involve a danger, and, without the discordant individuals even being conscious of their deficiency, the discordance can be weighed and eliminated in the general confrontation.

Reason does not dispense with corporeal concomitants. Without ceasing to be at the service of other drives and emotions, it tends partially to detach itself from them and to garner its own proper satisfactions. It originates from the relation, it is explained, expressed and maintained by, within, and for the relation. It belongs to the real, is fundamentally homogeneous with the whole of the real, and at present constitutes the greatest conscious grasp of the totality by one of its parts, or, as some of us say, of God and creation by man.[148] It contributes to bringing about happiness at once in the intellectual and profoundly affective grasp of the object, of the world, the other, the self, and even, for some, in the vision of God. Further, its exercise seems to be accompanied by a kind of feeling of well being linked to correct function, much like that which a hiker in good form can feel independently of the view. It has its rules, without which it would cease to be. There are compatibilities and incompatibilities, points of coherence and incoherence, hierarchies, choices. These are already evident in lower forms of life where they testify to an unconscious logic. They increase in consciousness in man and probably in many animals with what has come to be called the quest for satisfaction or the calculus of pleasures and pain, in order to blossom forth, not without continued struggle, along with the most authentic functions of the ego. In these activities and this transition we are crowning prior developments rather than seeking to negate them. We are trying to avoid the roles of both angel and brute, to set up prudent requirements for internal coherence, to proceed to a kind of enlightened calculus of happiness, without forgetting that it may just as well consist in providing happiness for others and that the application of the rule, effort, and struggle can add the color of their own proper satisfactions to the pleasures and happiness linked to ever wider and more free relations, bearing always in mind that a little foolishness is sometimes called for.[149] This evolution is favored or hampered by circumstances. It precedes the regression and dissolution of the person, or its transfiguration and survival in God. The memory of society or civilization can render the task easier or more difficult for the succeeding generations.

One important direction in the evolution of species is characterized by the increase in learned relations, in mobility, and in the freedom of the individual, by the qualitative enrichment of consciousness and at the same time by a proportionate increase in the neocortex of the brain.[150] It seems certain that some behaviors that are innate, partial, rigidly predetermined, and probably concomitant with some more obscure states of consciousness, are either disguised, controlled, utilized and transformed, or they disappear. As we have seen, this in no way entails any diminution in affectivity; simply put, the latter changes qualitatively while connoting relations of ever greater universality.

4   *Innate Behaviors, Maturation, Training, and Learning*

Multidisciplinary approach.
Briefly, innate behaviors would correspond to a sharply univocal explicitation of a defined and preadapted genetic script delivered complete at birth, and this explicitation would be independent of the circumstances in which the individual develops. This is not to say that these behaviors have no need of an internal maturation of the organism: that would be asking the egg to act like a bird. Nor does it mean that these behaviors are totally rigid: the triggering signs, also innate, can be common to situations that differ in other respects and constitute class distinctions.

For their part, learned behaviors would be no less instinctual and in a sense no less innate, but they would be so as virtualities, as an ability to learn. Their explicitation would be less sharply univocal, as much or more a function of present circumstances as of the genetic script. They would characterize the individual's adaptation, learning, and initiative, his ability to follow a fluid situation and to explore one given situation. Initially they would be grafted onto innate automatisms, at the service of basic needs, assisting in the steady improvement of their satisfaction by perfecting the relations between the internal and external poles of the drives. Then, without losing this primordial function, they would continue to develop more or less independently of it. Their mobility is not without conservation and memory: it is precisely this that is called learning. The remembrances gleaned in the course of the individual life would be more or less durable. In Darwinian theory, they would not exceed the lifetime of the individual and would not be transmitted to offspring. The Lamarckian theory has a different opinion on the point.

The comparative physiology of behavior, neurophysiology, psychology, and psychophysiology all demonstrate, throughout the course of the history of species and individuals, the graduated and progressive increase in the individual ability to learn. As the development of nerve structures goes on, the number of possible combinations increases: this is one of the corporeal aspects of the law of evolution in the tradition of Jackson and Teilhard de Chardin. The accoutrements of civilization, from the most primitive tools to computers, constitute so many instruments and prolongations of ourselves. Along with temporary connections, signs and signs of signs, Pavlovian reflexology insists upon the adaptibility of learning, and, as it were, upon its universality in some sense, since each perceptible variation in the environment can assume the value of a momentary efficacious sign. There is a certain noticeable utilitarianism at work here: everything learned conditionally is built upon innate behaviors and is at their service. Furthermore, this approach has not explored nonconditional acquisition, the enduring memory, the irreversible learning experiences, which, along with innate behaviors, constitute the solid framework of our development. Freud reveals to us the destiny of the drives, the beginnings of relationships and learning behaviors in the id, the influences of constraint and education which are soon introjected in the super-ego, and the formation of the ego. This last mentioned, the organ *par excellence* of reciprocal adaptation, would not escape the same accusation of utilitarianism levelled against conditional reflexes, should it be forgotten that at the same time it is the organ of highest consciousness and not totally given over to best satisfying primitive wants. For their part, philosophers and moralists have occasionally flirted with the contrary excess; in their eyes our ability to understand the world has sometimes eclipsed our more modest needs, more modest but no less fundamental: *primum vivere* . . . Finally, with the notions of genotype and phenotype, of degrees of liberty for the latter in respect to the former, of more or less univocal or plurivocal genetic actualization, more or less a function of the present environment, i.e., of exterior factors either aiding or impeding individual development—natural history encounters the old problems of potency and act, of virtuality and realization, of the relationships between the whole and the part . . .

Maturation, training, learning.

An innate behavior is characterized by the fact that it requires no preliminary learning. Success, i.e., reciprocal adaptation, takes place from the very beginning; the first stroke, as Corneille would have put it, is the stroke of a master: a bird raised in captivity, who has never seen a nest built, constructs its own as soon as the required internal and external conditions coincide; the spider spins its web without instruction. In our own species some behaviors of this kind have been observed at birth, in a pure state, so to speak: the first breath of air, ocular fixation and pursuit of a moving object set in contrast, a cry whose overtones of alarm are evident, even though at the beginning the child has no knowledge of them. Other organs and innate behaviors will be of use only later: limbs are present before there is any grasping or walking behavior; inversely, a bird flaps wings as if to fly when its wings are scarcely yet formed. The newborn child makes use of an extraordinarily rich range of facial expressions corresponding to the satisfaction or the nonsatisfaction of basic instinctual needs, to internal and external stimulations that the older child and the adult will call agreeable or disagreeable. The latter sometimes will employ this mimicry as a somewhat more conscious form of communication, unless it is purely and simply repressed, as in the apparent unperturbability of diplomats, Englishmen, or American Indians.[151][152] One and the same organ, or behavior structure, can be used in circumstances and with meanings that are markedly different: the newborn smiles when satiated or while sleeping; a little older, the nursing child smiles at the sight of a human face, be it that of a stranger or a grossly stylized mask; a little later it smiles in preference at its mother;[153] as for the older child and the adult, their smile indicates sympathy, friendship, love, humor, aggression, hate . . . Similar facts are observable in the evolution of species: the airbladder of a fish and the lungs of an airbreathing animal come from the same embryonic structure . . . This principle of economy or plasticity is an aspect of biological originality and relation, conservation and differentiation.

Granted that innate behaviors are defined by the fact that they require no learning, they are not, for all that, entirely present at the time of birth: they emerge successively during the course of development, as a certain internal maturation of the organism takes place. But reality is not so schematic. Learning, education and training intervene very early, sometimes already in the mother's womb: the excitation of the organs of equilibrium by the movements and positions of the mother, obstacles to the movements of the infant constituted by the wall of the sac, thumb sucking, absorption of amniotic fluid, etc. . . . their role is often difficult to evaluate, and all the more so in so far as they can bear upon not only the establishment of relation, the quest for satisfying situations and the avoidance of unsatisfactory situations, but also upon what the ethologist, reflexologists and psychoanalysts tend to consider as the internal pole of the drives, what is innate, instinctual, unconditional, absolute, or at least upon a part of that pole. The exercise of vision would hasten the myelinisation of the optic nerves. The child learns to sit, stand, walk, speak, to be clean, to manipulate objects, before acquiring professional competence and exercising itself in study, arts, sports, conflicts, struggles, love, pleasures . . . According to the quality of one's surroundings, maturation can be hastened or retarded, and regressions can occur.

However, within the limits of our present state of knowledge, the development of the main individual anatomical and functional structures which characterize our species cannot be hastened beyond a certain rate, nor can they transgress a certain order or overstep a certain point. This triple limitation, the third of which at least in some way runs counter to the idea of unlimited possible relations, points up the internal imperatives of maturation and attaches itself to other limitations. It is within this perspective that we must understand the neuroanatomical and behavioral changes that characterize, for example, the passage from the subcortical to the cortical level during the first months of life![154] [155] [156] The same considerations remain valid when the infant advances in age. The neuroanatomists show us nerve cells continuing to branch out in treelike fashion, the multiplication of their anatomical extensions and connections corresponding to the increase in possibilities of functional combinations. At the same time genetic epistemology shows us the progress of analysis and synthesis, the development of the understanding of real conservation, identity, succession, encasement, order, causality, the progress in interiority facilitating remembrance, prediction, reversibility, operations, and creative imagination.[157] The psychoanalytical concept of affective development gives just as much weight to the internal conditions of maturation as to exterior relations. It describes the normal or pathological affective development according to age and circumstances. It shows us that dependence and orality predominate during the course of the first months, followed by the appearance or an increase of independence, constraints and struggle with prehension and, above all, with the first steps and the learning of sphincter regulation,[158] the beginning of genital preoccupation, the age of reason overtaking that of the drives, of childhood obedience or disobedience . . . All of this does not take place haphazardly and without reference to a timeframe. It is not simply at the whim of exterior changes. There is a time to be born, a time to learn, a time to serve, a time to die. A man becomes a man, an ape does not become a man. Here we have other aspects of genetic constraints, protections and limitations.[159]

5   *The Liberty of Universality and*
Some Other Senses of the Word Liberty

The liberty of universality.
Liberty is first defined as a tendency toward universality, as a freedom of
movement for the individual, for the human being, allowing him finally to
know all, to understand all, to love all, without being entrapped or blinded
by anything. To the extent that it is impossible to do two different things at
once, to evolve at the same time in two different directions, the interest in the
whole is correlative with a certain detachment in respect to the part; this is
already observable in the most elementary psychophysiological manifestations.[160]

Several misunderstandings should be avoided. First, it is true that the
liberty of universality essentially implies the individual aptitude to learn and
understand, mobility throughout the depth and the breadth of the totality , in
contrast with the prefabricated, partial, rigid, and obscure character of
innate behaviors. But these latter, once understood, accepted, educated and
mastered in a suitable way, in the light of intelligence, constitute the
biological base, and, at the same time, a source of knowledge, activity, and
happiness. The same can be said for memory and acquired habits. Quite as
much as being hindrances, the elementary "automatisms," innate or acquired, can combine with mobility to constitute the condition of our liberty
and add to it a supplementary nuance. Second, universality does not mean a
kind of axiomatic stripped of everything sensible, a rarified or hollow
abstraction, but rather, in the purest sense of the French, the very meaning in
which Pascal and Descartes used the expression, the most concrete, i.e., the
most complete conscious grasp of the *res universa,* that is of the full and
entire reality. This improvement in consciousness makes use of all the
modalities of knowing—the senses and intelligence, analysis and synthesis;
it does not, however, effect coincidence between us and what we know, thus
preserving our own originality. Third, without thereby losing its significa-
tion of the fullest possible concreteness and entirety, it requires not so much
an extension as a deepening; one might better say that extension naturally

follows deepening: all beings cannot be explored individually, but each being leads us to understand others by way of analogy, and draws us to penetrate more or less profoundly the more or less deep, more or less common laws of reality. Finally, and not only for the above reason, universality does not neglect the part in behalf of the whole, primarily because the whole is nothing without its parts. But it locates the parts in respect to each other and to the whole, avoiding letting itself be imprisoned by any one part, allocating to each of them its proper place, appreciating it for what it is worth, using it without abusing it, and able to stop when necessary.

Other senses of the word "liberty."

The tendency toward liberty of universality is a simple fact of observation. We need only look to see its biological roots and its flowering or a beginning of its flowering in man. But the least observation shows us also that this tendency does not emerge equally in each individual, moment, or circumstance . . . There are some who express this acknowledged fact by saying that we have it in our power to tend or not to tend toward the Whole, the All, or God, to break our chains or to remain chained to what is limited or partial: that we are free, in the second sense of the word liberty, to free or not to free ourselves. But are we not thereby simply pushing back the problem and returning to a discussion of the notion of potency?

Whether they are extrapolating or transforming an observation about evolutionary direction into logical necessity, and the naturalists themselves do not lack motives for doing so, or for other reasons, a certain number of philosophers and theologians further hold that the tendency toward universality, "the determining power of the universal good," has a much greater force than the attraction of limited goods. For them the problem is not so much attraction to the part as refusal of the whole. They make of the latter the cause, the condition of the former, and, paradoxical as it may seem, the essential characteristic of what they call our free will. Men of bad will would use this power, plus fallen angels and their prince Satan (!), while moths and the stalks of plants would lack it in their irresistible quest for light. As for the damned, they would no longer be able to stop themselves from using this power, and even abusing it . . . At each instant, and in the most insignificant of his actions man would be able to direct his attention toward the sovereign good or refuse to do so; once having accepted it, he would be drawn toward it necessarily.[161] The question might be asked whether this does not bring about a somewhat artificial distinction between knowledge and behavior, contemplation and action, action and the focusing of attention, or whether the problem is not relegated to this last mentioned before being again deferred to the investigation of the notion of potency. As for Gabriel Marcel, he has made the observation that a number of our manifestations of universality appear not to happen at all according to the design of scholastic psychology, i.e., information, deliberation,[162] decision, and execution; instead they are often much more spontaneous, much less considered, I was about to say much more automatic.[163] And it is a matter of fact, quite undeniable, that drives toward reciprocal adaptation, expansion, service, good habits, etc., that are in a sense more obscure, play a considerable role here.

Others equate liberty with understood necessity, the impossibility of not lovingly conforming to the deep laws of reality once they come to consciousness.[164] With Socrates and Descartes they confuse ignorance with evil intent, but they do see that there are great obstacles which prevent this lived comprehension, and that in fact it is quite variable. For some it is creative inventiveness,[165] a project with no constraints except for those of reason.[166,167] For some, a pure and simple gratuitousness;[168] for others, doing what they please.[169] And for still others, liberty means free trade.[170]

Limiting our observations to things here below, we know very well that our tendency toward universality, our liberty in the first sense of the word, can be impeded, diminished or destroyed by genetic insufficiencies, malformations, illnesses, accidents, deprivations, excesses, toxic substances, old age, death . . . It manifests itself in varying degrees in accordance with age and individual, ethnic, or specific type, clearly not in the diversity of contemporary racial distinctions in the sense given by Gobineau[171] or, strangely, by Goebbels and Hitler, but throughout the course of the evolution of species, particularly that of the primates.[172] But above all our attention is more and more drawn to the social conditions of our blossoming forth: the affective quality of surroundings, education, instruction, economic conditions, nature, length and rhythm of work, spiritual atmosphere . . . What could be worse for the development of humanity in man than hunger, destitution, ignorance, totalitarianism, inquisition, faith expressed under force, the obligation of blind obedience, the crushing weight of inhuman labor, production and consumption gone wild? There are spaces where the spirit breathes freely, and there are other spaces where its breathing is stifled.

Is the phenotype, i.e., the real, concrete individual taken in existential fullness, exclusively the function of the environment, the external circumstances under which it develops, of the genetic code bestowed upon it by the evolution of species, and of possible mutations? Do other factors intervene? Should biologists write the biological formula for the individual: $P = f(G)(E)$, or $P = f(G)(E)(?)$? In order to respond to this question it would be advisable to employ the accepted method of varying each factor separately, or at least those that are known and with which we can deal. Supposing identical twins are endowed with an identical genetic potential, how would they develop if they are educated in different conditions? What would happen to genetically different individuals, different in type, race, species, potential for anomalies, etc., who are raised under identical conditions? This kind of study frequently presents great difficulties: mutations aside, we are not dealing with genetically pure races of men; our rhythm of growth and reproduction is relatively slow; differences within the environment are often difficult to appreciate and master, and reciprocal influences can lead to an almost geometric progression in the amplification of these differences.[173] But here again we must be wary of letting the trees hide the forest. If necessary, evolution and social revolutions alone would show us the virtualities with which the so-called races of slaves were endowed.

The better we know genetic and environmental determinations, the narrower the margin for other possible factors. Finally, once again we see that the notion of virtualities, of potencies, of a multiplicity or univocity of "possible" realizations, differs to the extent that either the part or the whole is under consideration. A virtuality that is multiple from the perspective of the part is perhaps unique in light of the whole. Were the need for reciprocal adaptation and the chance of genetic mutations the only factors involved, the problem would doubtlessly remain unchanged since chance is not an indetermination.

Neurotic obstacles to the liberty of universality. Unconscious analogical repetitions.

The practice of psychiatry puts us in daily contact with neurotic patients, that is prisoners of learned, rigid, inappropriate triggering signs and reacting behaviors, in brief of bad habits. Their cure constitutes a kind of abbreviated evolution of the person in the direction of liberty of universality, of liberation in the first meaning of the word liberty: being neither blinded nor trapped by the part, being able to understand the whole, follow a changing situation, explore a given situation in all its ramifications, order parts in relation to other parts and to the whole. Perhaps these facts further afford us some additional indications relative to the second sense of the word, the liberty to free oneself or to remain a prisoner.

A behavior that is neurotic at the present time could have once been adapted, logical, and genuine. At the same time the little girl needs her mother, is constrained by her, does not enjoy the same rights as she does, loves her, depends on her, dislikes her and fears her all the more for that, feels frustrated, restrained, inferior, aggressive and guilty. She correctly evaluates the situation and, in a sense, reacts in the appropriate way. If familial and social circumstances are favorable, if the mother is sufficiently attractive and clever and if the father knows how to make the correct allowances and counterallowances, then in the absence of other obstacles the child will gradually acquire the liberty of judgment and action of a mentally healthy adult.

In the contrary case we can be faced with the fixation of an infantile behavior. As circumstances change this behavior becomes progressively unrelated, ill-adapted, ineffective, illogical, wrong. In every new situation the patient is sensitive to one certain sign only, and reacts to it always in the same way. This learned triggering sign generally consists in an element common to the original situation and to subsequent situations which often differ from it considerably in other respects, and which frequently exhibit only the weakest kind of analogy with it. The common domain is sometimes extremely tenuous, vague, or general. Eventually any human relation can set the automatic repetition into motion. One of my patients had unresolved feelings of hostility toward her mother. She felt threatened simply by my presence, substituting me for her mother and transfering to me all her old and still current feelings for her. She insulted me coarsely and violently about whether I spoke, what I said, and whether I remained silent. To these were added other displays such as identification with the aggressor, projection of her own drives onto the other, the directing of her own aggressiveness towards herself, etc. . . .

It is possible that the learned triggering sign is not always an element common to initial and current situations. Perhaps the Pavlovian notion of a sign of a sign, i.e., of a sign of the nth degree, must be introduced, but with greater rigidity and inertia than the normal conditional connection, which is basically temporary; it could be that structuralism and reflexology complement rather than oppose each other. At least, it is advisable not to forget that here structuralism has only a descriptive and partially explanatory value. The causal, genetic point of view introduces other explanatory elements, such as ambient conditions and an eventual typology, which generate fixations.[174] Nor should we forget that in certain modalities of individual memory conditioning does no more intervene than in innate, instinctual behaviors, which do not require any learning.

Just as on the instinctual level, the neurotic patient is imprisoned within a forced, automatic, rigid, stereotyped, partial, obscure behavior, which is triggered by a sign whose situation within the whole is not seen; certainly learning did take place, but it became precociously fixated, a little like the process of "imprinting" described by the ethologists.[175] To be overwhelmed by a detail from the past, analogically felt and lived in all subsequent situations, is equivalent to being unfree in respect to the whole. Not only is the subject unconscious of this, but, in a certain way, he is equally unaware that his behavior is pathological; he is, as they say, *anosognosic*. One of the characteristics of his illness is his lack of ability to make comparisons. It is a little as if he were bound face forward against a tree: he sees neither the forest nor the tree itself. Yet, in another way, the unconsciousness can fall short of being total. There can be some tics that are almost completely unconscious, but most often neurotic behaviors are accompanied by a certain consciousness, sometimes nuanced by a vague sense of inadaptation, speciousness, incongruity, error, and failure. Along with the suffering and pain, the obsessions and what have come to be called psychosomatic conversion symptoms are often the only motives that draw a patient to seek counseling.

Comparison between neurotic automatisms and epileptic automatisms.
Epileptic automatisms exhibit some similarities. In Penfield's "experiential responses," electrographically registered paroxysms supervening at the level of the temporal cortex are accompanied by a forceful invasion of the mind by an hallucinatory recollection, which is frequently repetitive during spontaneous epileptic seizures, less often during neurosurgical exploration, at least when the electrode does not remain stationary during the successive electrical stimulations. During the hallucination the patient involuntarily fixes his attention on it and loses touch with his actual situation. The cases are rare in which he can halt the unfolding of the critical automatism by thinking of something else ("psychical arrest"); in the absence of treatment the contrary normally takes place.[176]

The resemblances between epileptic and neurotic automatisms become even more striking in the case of certain patients suffering from both temporal epileptic and neurotic seizures. In such cases, we can see the same stereotyped pattern, the same repetitive thought content, the same, always identical behavior showing up during an epileptic seizure as well as during their habitual neurotic acting out.[177] But despite a certain resemblance, and even an occasional coincidence, these two orders of symptoms present differences. The epileptic automatisms are in a sense less coessential with the relational development; the subject may be imprisoned by his seizures, but between them his ego can appear strongly developed. To the contrary, neurotic automatisms are basically rooted in the persistence of infantile ways of feeling and reacting.

It is impossible to be absorbed by a detail and at the same time understand the whole; in this sense stereotyped automatism and liberty are mutually exclusive.[178] At least we might ask whether there is a *primum movens*. Is it the force of the epileptic or neurotic automatism that blocks the higher activities, or is it the momentary or enduring weakness of the latter or a deficiency in their development that "frees" the automatism? Or is there correlation without causal precedence?

Basing himself principally on a study of epilepsy conducted with the means at his disposal, Jackson made of automatisms in general a positive symptom of liberation for activities of a lower level. By this he meant that higher controls were suppressed, i.e., that it was an inhibiting of inhibition.[179] And, really, there is hardly any other explanation for a major cortical seizure than a local inhibition. Further, the subsequent resection of a cortical zone does not destroy a remembrance previously evoked during an electrical paroxysm produced in that area. The remembrance, however, does not invade the field of consciousness as it did during the seizures, before that region of the cortex presumed to inhibit habitually the remembrance and to be itself inhibited pathologically at times, was surgically suppressed. We run up against our ignorance regarding the location and nature of the mnemonic traces, an ignorance that is complicated by the duplication of cerebral hemispheres and, in the words of Penfield, by the almost complete mystery surrounding hypothetical cortical inhibitions in general.[180] Nothing authorizes us to exclude the possibility of a direct stimulation of anatomical and functional "patterns" presumed to correspond to remembrance. The succesful action of sedatives, starting with the revered bromide and phenobarbital, can be invoked in favor of both hypotheses: indeed, these substances can weaken the automatism, but they possibly do the same with the inhibition of its inhibition. All that is known for certain is that the cortical spikes diminish, and the pathological symptoms too.

In the case of neurotics one rather tends to invoke as *primum movens* the force of bad habits, which in turn is possibly related to an inert and obstinate typology, whether hereditary or acquired early in life, and certainly to the violence, abruptness, prolongation, and repetition of the affects at work during the initial pathogenic situations (to, as Pavlov maintained, the overloading and collision of excitement), as well as to other circumstances, e.g., continued insufficiency in the infant's surroundings, mistakes and gaps in education and instruction, ignorance, obscurantism . . . Weakness in the development of the ego would initially be a consequence rather than a cause, but in its turn would create aggravation. Here again it is not always easy to detect a chronology in correlative events.[181]

Treatment of neuroses. Improvement of insight, modification of transference, accessory means. Prophylaxis.

Experience shows that it is useless to appeal to the will of a neurotic patient in the sense of a direct fight against his pathological automatisms. Even if he is aware of them, he is just as defenseless against them when they are happening as an epileptic in the throes of an hallucinatory seizure; what is more, by accusing him of lack of will power we increase his guilt and his morbid symptoms, just as can happen if we scold a child with a nervous twitch. Sometimes this sickness of the will, or inability to act according to reason at certain times and in certain matters, along with the ability to do so in others, is not entirely unconscious. The patient will frequently say such things as, "I know it's crazy, but I can't stop myself." This is particularly striking when the patient is undergoing appropriate therapy, gaining better understanding of the meaning of his neurotic automatisms, and starts to free himself from them somewhat. When pathological repetition takes place, trapping the patient, everything else is once again forgotten for the moment: the new relationships that are more adult, freer, and more broad, the new interests, even the meaning of the automatism itself. What Freud called the persistence of the forces of repression indicates that neither the illness nor the treatment is at an end.[182] It would be more exact to say, "When I happen to behave as I did before, I start by forgetting everything. I am no longer aware of any absurdity." The neurotic automatism and the consciousness of it as such are mutually exclusive, and there is no willing without consciousness. The analogy inherent to neurotic forms of behavior compounds the strength of habit and repressive factors and makes the act of consciousness both difficult and, initially, precarious: during analogical repetitions, identity becomes clouded by the differences. The desire to take medical advice, begin and continue treatment, is rooted in the healthy, reasonable and well adjusted part of the personality, in moral encouragement and eventual material assistance from those about him, as well as in certain modalities of initially unconscious transference, such as dependence, infantile obedience and love, stubbornness, etc. . . .

It is similarly deceiving to want to cure a neurotic patient by trying to interest him in "something else," in having him travel, or change his environment: while he is prey to his repetitive automatism, nothing else in the world really interests him except his own unsolved problems, and nothing else captures his vision and activity so intensely. This does not mean that certain defensive mechanisms such as avoidance, isolation, compulsive work, obsessions, rationalization, opposition, and doubt, are necessarily devoid of positive elements; if these exist, however, they are nuanced by a general neurotic flavor surrounding the relational life of the subject. Nor, we repeat, does it mean that the patient cannot demonstrate a certain willingness to be cured, nor that education and instruction do not play a fundamental role in the prevention and even the cure of neuroses: is not the principal task of psychotherapy to help the patient understand himself? Man grasping hold of himself from within, is this not one of the highest forms of knowing, both in object and method?

According to our present state of knowledge, the most effective therapeutic methods confirm this opinion that the strength of old behaviors dominates the arrest of development. Again, there is no question of telling the patient "you can, you should, you should not, you must, you must not." No more is it a question of ordering him to open his eyes and look around. First and foremost, the repetitive automatism is the objective. This is the object in the projector's focus, and it is a matter of directing awareness towards it by analyzing the past and present way of being in existence in general and transference in particular. Taking direction from what has come to be called the free association of ideas, from dreams, from behavior, the physician labors perseveringly to clear away that which constantly tends to hide the perpetual, analogical repetition from the patient: forgetfulness, the repression of initial situations that are from the distant past and poorly understood, painful and frightening, and the differences among successive situations, circumstances, and reactions right down to present experience, differences which serve to mask the morbid identity. This difficult grasp of one's neurotic automatisms, when it happens, does more to modify them than any encouragement or attraction, or at least what is considered in life to be attractive for mentally healthy people. This clarification of the unhealthy behavior and the consequent change work best in transference, that is, in a present existential relationship one of whose terms, the psychotherapist, understands what is happening and explains it to the patient. As the understanding and the lessening of the pathological repetition go on, human relationships change in character, the world brightens, and the zest for true life arises.

Thus the cure for these unconscious, uncontrollable, analogical repetitions known as neuroses is basically associated with the improvement of the insight and the modification of the transference, i.e.,by psychoanalytical psychotherapy under its various forms.[183] There is an increasing tendency to facilitate this process by additional and temporary forms of assistance, initially by chemical means. These, in their turn, aim at lessening the force of the neurotic automatism. It seems they should be applied under very precise rules. They should favor an awareness and a modification of the transference that continue once the medication has stopped. They should permit certain critical moments to be surmounted, such as those in which the patient presents a grave danger to himself or others, and for that reason would have otherwise needed to be committed to psychiatric internment. Other such critical moments are the situation in which the violence of a negative repetition during transference might lead to a rejection or interruption of psychotherapy, that in which repression, resistance, or inhibition opposes an overwhelming obstacle, or the case in which shattered neurotic defenses leave a still weak ego in the grip of the real and understandably alarming dangers surrounding the struggle for life. These chemical aids should be used only in cases of extreme necessity, and in the smallest dosage effective. They should not mask symptoms, give illusory assurance, hinder transference, nor result in an indefinite dependence on physicians and drugs. During analysis the psychiatrist is particularly able to deliberate and decide upon what medicine to use, the dosage, when it should be administered, and when it should be abandoned.[184]

Situational and social changes that happened during treatment can assist in the growth of awareness, if no more than by helping answer possible questions about what arises from the patient and what from his surroundings. By themselves, at least after a certain age, they seem unable to modify deep affective habits. They run the risk of acting out, of collapse of the transference, irreversible decisions, etc. . . . Often, when they escape analysis, they succeed only in once again substituting for former situations and reactions analogous situations and reactions. This is what social therapy seeks to avoid, from psychodrama and group psychotherapy to the least artificial modifications of the environment. One might speculate whether deconditioning, for its part, is not limited by the fact that one part of this abnormal memory called neurotic might very well escape conditioning mechanisms, or at least those of usual conditioning, which is basically provisional. As for neurosurgery, lobotomy or other operations, for now they are grossly disfiguring; the cure is worse than the disease.

Prophylaxis depends on social conditions, customs, lifestyles, forms of civilization, instruction, education, and on the mental health of the educators. Early prophylactic and curative methods are based upon a human relationship that is rapidly and increasingly impregnated with consciousness, upon friendship, example, and true explanation. This in no way excludes a certain amount of training and the prudent, selective use of the fear of punishment and the promise of reward, which is also a calculus of pleasure and pain. The principal problems remain those of the will to power, aggressiveness, and sexuality.[185]

In short, faced with a neurotic patient, the physician at no time has the impression that he is treating someone free to choose or to reject freedom, or for whom the very words choice and freedom have any meaning. The automatic repetition that impedes the establishment of a comprehensive and true relationship with reality is generally unconscious. The attraction of the whole, as some philosophers say, is insufficient to "superdetermine" him, even for consultation and the acceptance of and perseverance in treatment. We should not labor under illusions; our patients do not consciously come to us seeking liberty, but rather the cessation of some vague discomfort. Often there are the modalities, initially unconscious, of the transference, and the attitude of one's social milieu, which favor the continuation of treatment. When it is successful, and other circumstances permitting, the person is rewarded by that which he was not even capable of perceiving and seeking: the liberty of universality and the happiness coessential with it.

Education for liberty.

Teachers themselves are not limited to the giving of instruction. At the same time that they form our taste for beauty, truth and universality while *showing,* that is, while informing, teaching, and instructing, they train us and rectify within us that which opposes these tendencies. They should be able to discern pathological blocks. Like each of us, they should not fear to face up to outside obstacles. Among the most glaring of these are the exploitation of man by man, inhuman labor, the delegation of reason, unbridled consumption, and different kinds of pollution, beginning with noise and carbon dioxyde from cars.[186] [187] [188] [189]

The liberty of universality does not spring up *ex nihilo,* or as if an intellectual, immortal soul were unceremoniously grafted onto the body of an animal. To begin with, reason serves extremely primitive modalities of reciprocal adaptation. Even when it partially disengages from them, this transformation proceeds by way of conservation and emergence much more than through the pure and simple destruction of what precedes. Utilitarianism, defensive rationalization, more or less illusory reassurances, identification, surpassing, the affirmation of adult manhood or femininity, narcissism, the need to be admired, sexuality, hierarchy, territory, the will to power, compensations, the spirit of service, the sense of rhythm, of repetition, order, geometric beauty, deepening, and perfection, if not typology or obsessional defenses . . . such are, more or less affected by disguises, displacement, substitution, sublimation, shading our relational instinct, some of the roots of our interest in all beings, as well as of our worst hindrances, depending on circumstances. We also need to take all of these into account.

Education towards freedom regarding the part, towards interest in the whole, the extirpation of limiting automatisms, the suppression of external obstacles do not, for all that, mark an end to the fight; humanity within us merely finds itself less defenseless. Another way consists in taking advantage of moments of greater detachment in order to side step, as much as possible, certain traps; these may not be actually and comparatively very attractive, but they might manifest all their force if approached too closely and touched, as it is said, with no more than the tip of a finger. At least, we ought not to be mistaken about the definition of pitfalls, nor to continue in or fall back upon the obscure defenses of the child and the sick man. It is a sad life indeed, and how imprisoning, for one who fights against his most legitimate, most necessary, and least enslaving satisfactions: take, for example, the man who, like Anthony, would go lock himself away in the desert in the belief that he was escaping his swinish urges, or someone who would play at blind obedience, or put on the disguise of a mendicant . . . Nevertheless, even when the struggle between our tendency towards universality and our contrary tendencies proceeds as a more equal contest, and even when, assisted by means and ruses like those we have described, we more usually are progressing towards our richest humanity, experience shows that we can still be subject to relapses, regressions, and set-backs: in the domain of spiritual progress, as well, the Tarpeian rocks are close to the Capitols. The fight goes on to the end.

What more are we now able to say about liberty in the second sense of the word, that of becoming free from detail or remaining locked into it, of the ability or lack of ability to move throughout the whole with the required ease, consistency, and coherence? There is no doubt that we know a little more about some of the circumstances that impede the growth of the liberty of universality within us. But do we know all of them? And if we were to know all of them, would it be possible for us not to do away with them? Would we not be under the compulsion of the liberty of universality and the happiness that it brings? Would there remain any ability to refuse? The question seems far from resolved, even though it is correctly posed.

One fact stands out. Despite progress in social organization, material well-being, teaching, education, and mental hygiene, at least in countries called civilized, tendencies contrary to those which appear to characterize humanity in man continue to emerge. There is a certain mediocrity, a certain stunting, that mark the badly distributed, insufficient, exaggerated, or inappropriate consumption of material goods. Alcoholism continues to rage. Countless young people use drugs. Workers are alienated and dehumanized for another's profit. Men are transformed into the cogs of a machine. Collective organizations that, paradoxically, deny individual worth to the individual members which compose them, spring into existence. New dogmas and new inquisitions succeed the old ones, continuing to "hate furiously the man who seeks knowledge." What is more, just as much as spiritual growth, these regressions often appear to take place deliberately and in the full light of consciousness. But before casting suspicion on the mysterious third factor, the willing of good or evil, the power of saying yes or no, the freedom of liberating or not liberating oneself and others, it behooves us to make an even more complete analysis of circumstances. Examples of this kind of analysis have already been given. Some others, dealing with economic and cultural problems, will be found in the fourth part of this work.

6   *Individual, Group, Species*

The originality of the individual and the originality of the group.
To say, as does modern genetic theory, that the phenotype, or realized individual, is a function of the genotype and the environment, is to say that it is a nexus of relations: past relations in which the genotype persisted and was differentiated, and present relations in which the individual is formed and possibly experiences new mutations. We made guarded mention of the hypothetical existence of a third factor, "liberty" in the second sense of the word. A large part of these relations are of a social order.

If the individual is a nexus of relations, this does not mean that he is reducible to the sum of these relations, just as the properties of water are not reducible to the sum of the properties of hydrogen and oxygen. The same holds true for society. At first society certainly takes its quality from that of each of its members, but in no way is it reducible to their sum. Two men can move a load that neither one could move by himself: their forces combine with each other; yet it is necessary that they avoid working against each other, and that, perhaps by prior agreement, one of them takes command. Some of the social characteristics involved are division of labor, organization, hierarchization, collective memory, tradition, civilization, contestation, and statistical or other laws proper to the group.

One must not confuse the levels of evolution, the types of originalities. It can only be in metaphor that we speak of collective consciousness and of the body social, to say nothing of the bosom of France,[190] the eye of Moscow, the ear of the pope, or the secular arm. Such symbolism is not necessarily without artistic value or power of analogical suggestion, but it often skirts the ridiculous even when there is no risk of being taken literally, inducing error, or scandalizing. We sympathize with the linguistic difficulties experienced by the clergy and their parishioners wrestling with different, mixed symbolisms: pastors and flocks, members of the Church in communion with the Body of Christ, identified individually and as a group with Him who is their head and spouse . . . Many of our brothers prefer to speak more simply, if not always more judiciously, of the people of God, of the elect, or the Chinese, the German race, human kind, classes, etc.

From the most elementary sexuality that does not even need an encounter between gamete bearers, to the most evolved forms of civilization, the variety of social groups and behaviors is beyond measure. They are not identical with species. One is even hesitant to consider them as aspects of species when one reflects upon the importance, among certain social groups, of guests belonging to other species. The notion of species results, if you will, from an "analogical abstraction." It is a class title.

Comparative duration of individuals and groups, and of some of their effects.

The relationships between the lifespans of individuals and that of social entities are extremely variable. Sometimes, as in brief sexual encounters, transitory associations, and nonviable political regimes, the lifespan of the individual exceeds that of the society. Normally the contrary happens: in the biological sense, the life of the individual is relatively ephemeral. Some believe in immortality of the soul, in the resurrection of the flesh, in an eternal life, happy or unhappy depending upon our works here below. Others do not believe in such things and strive all the harder to prolong our earthly life.[191] Others, setting a stout heart against bad luck, prefer their lives "short and sweet;" that, however, depends on what one chooses to call fullness, and despite everything it is well to recall that nothing much is done without time. No doubt, our distant descendants will look upon us as sacrificed generations who die in infancy before the age of a hundred . . . Still others, along with the old Epicureans, observe that while we are, death is not, and when death occurs, we no longer are: the twain, therefore, shall not meet, and our lifespan, short as it is, takes on a kind of eternity since, on our dying day, time, for us, ceases to be. Obviously we can quibble about the words, but the idea is not an empty one; it also gives our short life a kind of absolute value and has provided comfort to a large number of us.

It has been observed that among the majority of living beings there exists a propensity to devote oneself to others, while at the same time perduring and growing, no matter whether this propensity is conscious or unconscious, innate or learned, more or less violently imposed by the group, more or less quietly introjected, more or less justified rationally. These two tendencies are at once in opposition and in support of one another. One gives in the measure that he has and is, and giving contributes to self-realization. Christianity recognizes this well when it recommends that we love our neighbor as ourselves, when it affirms that without charity we are but "sounding brass,"[192] that he who would save his soul will lose it, and that well ordered charity begins with oneself. Initially the young Freud showed less understanding of this when he radically opposed the sexual tendencies, as basically serving the interest of the species, to the ego drives, directed towards self-preservation.

In the total world of living beings, the activity of individuals often has consequences that outlast them, and not only in the vague or general sense that there is nothing in the universe unrelated to what preceded it or follows it. Reproduction, infant care and other social behaviors favor the perpetuation, progress and evolution of the group and of the species. Whether we like it or not, we give a large part of ourselves to other people and other things, helping them endure longer than ourselves: to our children, our families, groups, associations, classes, places, mother countries, societies, churches, works of charity, various causes . . . We have no alternative but to recognize a great apparent similarity in our ways of being, whether or not we believe ourselves immortal in the religious sense of the word. We have the same solicitude for ourselves and for others, for the development of persons, institutions, and civilization. It is as if, beneath different theoretical constructions and languages, a community of instincts, of "nature" were expressing itself . . . We can scarcely blame those who believe in paradise for occasionally neglecting this "vale of tears," this place of passage which nonetheless has need for a minimum of material goods in order to enable man to develop spiritually, nor can we blame those who do not believe for sometimes undervaluing the individual, who passes so quickly as compared with more durable, collective realizations, forgetting that although a collectivity differs in part from the sum of its members it is, nevertheless, nothing without them. One can further suppose that one of the first effects of a prolongation of life for the individual will be a lessening of reproduction, if it is true that there is less room for men on earth than in heaven and that a certain growth excludes a certain multiplication. It is possible that quality will then replace quantity, and that the future of the species and the group will coincide in a greater degree with that of the individual. But what will remain of the sexual instinct when it becomes sytematically disassociated from procreation? The problem is already present. Our academicians, for their part, call themselves immortal on the grounds that they think, rightly or wrongly, that their effects in the world will be particularly important and durable.

Learned and innate social behaviors. Reconsideration of a difficulty with the Darwinian theory. Some sources of morality and religion.
Whether ways of being between husband and wife, parents and children, brothers and sisters or betweeen other social partners, or those involved in hierarchy, territory, battle, competiton, or mutual assistance, a large number of our biological behaviors, innate or learned, are social behaviors.[193 194]

Except for mutations, let us recall that entirely innate behaviors emerge completely developed through the phylogeny. They demand a certain degree of internal maturation, indeed, a certain amount of exercise, but they dispense with learning. They are preadapted, i.e., adapted immediately when the triggering and satisfying situations are those in which they were formed during the course of the evolution of species. The inadaptability of the individual, its failure to understand the whole of the situation, what we are sometimes tempted to call its stupidity, becomes visible when the triggering signs are disassociated from usual conditions. Excluding it from all learning, it is this kind of behavior that the entomologist Fabre, probably with some exaggeration, attributed to insects.[195] If they are truly innate, in their complexity and perfection these behaviors are almost more surprising than internal adaptation, and perhaps even more than the possibilities of a neuronic combination so vast in our species that it corresponds to our power to know the world. Would one solitary wasp, completely unconscious of the consequences of its act, entomb together its egg and a paralyzed caterpillar to feed its larva? No matter how the Darwinian theory explains that the number of chance mutations has been literally enormous throughout the course of geological time, there remains the difficulty of showing that such encounters and their selection had some probability . . . This is why the ancient zoologists had a tendency to make instinctual behaviors a heritage of intelligent ancestors, or an accumulation of successive, individual learning experiences; but they in their turn run up against major difficulties, such as the inheriting of learned characteristics.

During the course of the evolution of individuals and of species, exploratory activities come to be grafted onto innate behaviors. The individual searches out triggering and satisfying situations, and in this quest he employs ever greater ingenuity and intelligence. He educates and diversifies his pleasures, and sometimes even his discomforts . . . at least that which causes others discomfort.[196] He becomes more and more able to foresee, to calculate habitually so as to obtain more pleasure than displeasure. He learns, either alone or with the help of society. This instruction, education, tradition, and civilization, communicated to each of us through the community appear or suddenly develop in our species in direct correlation with the increase in our individual intellectual potential as well as the increase in possibilities for collective memory, logic, and communication. There is another process, whose roots already appear in other species, that starts to blossom forth in our own. While one part remains at the service of more primitive instincts, of other vital needs, our intelligence becomes partly detached from them. Our science and practice, our desire for power, for having and knowing, for contemplating and acting, all these open themselves upon the world and, along with them, our social relationships.

In its main outlines, the evolution of species certainly involves a relative increase in learning behavior. But we have seen that it is often difficult to distinguish what is innate and what is learned, to decide, as modern geneticists put it, whether the explicitation of the individual genetic patrimony is strongly or weakly univocal. The study of learning among "instinctual" animals is still not very advanced, and it probably holds more than one surprise in store for us. Inversely, we are beginning to detect that beneath human morality that is apparently or truly of the highest rationality there lurks, without doubt, a number of behaviors that are innate in the strictest sense of the term, as well as learning behaviors that are in a way unconscious: introjected social examples, prescriptions, and taboos, which psychoanalysts call the super-ego. This is not to imply that such morals are ill-adapted, illogical, or erroneous. Nor does it mean that they cannot be examined freely by the light of the authentic rationality of the ego, and then be accepted, perfected, modified, or refused. But, in the general Hegelian perspectives which we have already discussed, this could illustrate the progressive grasp of the mutual agreement and logic of things by human reason, of the whole by the part, of reality by man.[197] Is not this something like what Gabriel Marcel was alluding to when he referred to the approbation that we might give *a posteriori* to acts that were at once "spontaneous," without reflection, and good? And what Bergson spoke of in the matter of the different "sources of morality and religion"?[198] To what are possibly examples of the spirit of humility or cosmic communion as observed by Darwin and Mrs. van Lawick-Goodall,[199] we might add the numberless manifestations of the spirit of service and social assistance throughout the world of animals. Even in the domain of morals and religions, this spirit of service, let us note in passing, does not exclude a certain amount of combat and of solitude

Rigidity, mobility, partiality, concretude, and universality within individual and social behaviors.

Rigidity is first noticed within innate behaviors: the organism always reacts in the same way to the same sign, all else being equal on the side of internal conditions, other signs, and other innate behaviors. For its part, learning is at once mobile and rigid, involving both exploration and memory. It remains largely at the service of innate, rigidly defined biological activities. These mixed behaviors, so to speak, are mobile at one end and fixed in the other. Once it escapes primitive needs learning still takes place through conservation and emergence and according to specific type. In every case it relies on individual memory. If conditioning has roots in more or less temporary connections, other modalities of learning are more basically durable, in the sense that what has been learned is not forgotten, at least until the onset of disease or old age. In individual evolution as in the evolution of the species, remembrance of the past is the condition of present life and future conquests. Collective memory—a term perhaps acceptable less metaphorically than collective consciousness (we speak as well of a computer's memory, but not of its consciousness)—partakes of the memory of the species and that of the individual, while at the same time adding to them. Without these social means of conservation there would be no human development.

Partiality, i.e., the fact that the whole is not taken into account, but only the part, operates with rigidity as well as mobility, with innateness as well as with learning. The repetitive character of an innate behavior, habit, or neurotic automatism exemplifies rigid partiality; the subject sees only a tiny part of reality, that which the history of the species or its own history has appointed for it, and he always reacts to it in the same way. As for the patient suffering from Korsakow's dementia, he is entirely given over to the present moment. All is forgotten from one moment to the next; nothing is fixed, and the patient flits from one object to the next; it would be a perfect *carpe diem*, if only pleasure itself, as Socrates felt, did not require some minimum of memory . . . Concretude, completeness, and universality themselves demand permanence and change, mobility and fixity, conservation and emergence, exploration and memory. Such, as we have seen, are some of the main characteristics of the dialectic of the real in general and particularly that of man, of human thinking.

At the same time, depending on the way in which rigidity and mobility, partiality and concretude, tradition and initiative are brought into combination, some outstanding social types acquire broad outlines. There are societies in which the univocal genetic relations predominate, where each member perceives in his fellow only a narrow mosaic of innate signs operating each in its turn, or which combine with each other, oppose each other, interfere with each other in different ways.[200] [201] [202] [203] There are consuming societies where intelligence is reduced to its utilitarian function in the most primitive sense, ordered entirely to the satisfaction of basic instincts. There are societies with traditions of intolerance, of inquisitions and *autos-da-fé*, which allow no development or development only within narrow dogmatic cadres. There are societies in which the criteria of a certain social preferment are an ultra-mobile conditioning, a "plasticity." There are entirely militaristic societies, gigantic postal and telecommunications networks worthy of the *"Grand-Guignol,"* in which each member tends to be transformed into a soldier who obeys blindly, or a mailman who transmits messages with no knowledge of their content.[204] There are societies in which the individual in relationship is educated for initiative and liberty, which in turn would profit the others taken individually and as a group.[205]

Persons and societies of persons. Unity and diversity. Some choices and consequences.

Even though an object of attention for certain religions,[206] the notion of human person has nothing theological, metaphysical, or otherwise mysterious about it. It expresses a simple matter of fact in natural history: zoologists, who include themselves within it, assign to the human species a certain number of living organisms in so far as they display an exceptionally elevated degree of rational tendency, i.e., at once logical and conscious, towards order and universality. Initially it matters little to the naturalist that this tendency be an awakening of consciousness of the totality in one of its parts, a desire of the microcosm to incorporate the macrocosm into itself, or a participation in God or an image of God . . . He is hardly at all concerned whether these ways of expression bear any fundamental resemblances. He is no longer embarrassed by the existence of contrary tendencies and realizations in us: he is satisfied to note them, describe them, and to make the observation that, from the perspective of zoological classification, they lessen humanity in man. He has some reasons to think that the tendency towards humanization, in the sense noted above, plunges its roots deeply into biological evolution, and that it will persist and grow in perfection, and along with it our species. Other observations, however, could raise some doubts about that: for example, the observation of a tendency, no less primitive and tenacious, of delegating understanding and power, if not that of each member to all members (which is probably meaningless), at least that of the majority of members to some of them; of a tendency to certain divisions of labor and to certain social organizations from which are constantly born and reborn new races of masters, as Mao Tse-tung said. But the naturalist also perceives that the individual is nothing without relation and without its group. He observes the mutual support that helps man to remain man, to become more manlike, and to go beyond himself, as Nietzsche said, without for all that ceasing to be man.

How are we to reconcile our tendency towards universality with our limitations? Do not the latter make of the former an illusion, a decoy? Whatever be our gifts,[207] our health, our longevity, social progress, it remains that none among us, alone or with one's group, will ever be able to do or to know everything, that work will inevitably continue to require division, and that our individual originality, if truly a nexus of relations, will continue to result in part from chance encounters. How else but by a hollow, fallacious, and hypocritical abstraction, are we to reconcile humanity and diversity among men?[208] On the other hand, to the degree that men progress in concrete universality and in awareness of the whole, do they not thereby tend to efface their individual differences and conserve only their specific originality: conscious logic and truth, i.e., reason, being man's accord with himself and things, understood necessity, the same for all? Do they not necessarily tend towards an elevated levelling through the unity of the whole, through the totality? Such is, considered in some of its bearings, the problem of individual ways of spiritual development. It straightway evokes three kinds of observations: one concerning the relationships between culture and the diversity of its approaches, another concerning proportion and lack of pretentiousness, and a third concerning theoretical and practical concepts of justice and choice.

The movement, progress and conquests of concrete thinking, we repeat, do not require that each atom be known and acted upon: this would burden us with an overwhelming impossibility. But, in a certain way, each time that we know or act upon a tiny part of the universe it may implicate and increase our knowledge of the entire universe. Knowing and perfecting oneself, understanding and aiding those about us, paying attention to one's immediate surroundings and acting upon them, these can often serve to understand the world better than travelling its length and breadth. This suggests the sense in which the philosophers of antiquity spoke of each being as able to assist us in grasping Being and other beings. The humblest of our concrete approaches, our trade, profession, work, and daily rounds, can open us to the goods of civilization at the same time as we contribute to them. The division of labor and the diversity among people, far from necessarily involving an impoverishment of the individual, can be a factor in the spiritual enrichment of each and of all. Bookish culture can be hollow: *"Habe nun, ach! Philosophie, Juristerei und Medizin und leider auch Theologie durchaus studiert, mit heissem Bemühn. Da steh ich nun, ich armer Tor, und bin so klug als wie zuvor!"*—so exclaimed Faust before loving Marguerite and becoming an engineer. Recall Mao Tse-tung's attempt to unite industrial labor, agricultural labor, and studies, at all levels.[209] Nevertheless, without even speaking of dogmatic frameworks, one of the risks which we see all too often in our own country is the confusion betweeen culture and technology; it is true that there are stages and priorities.

It is nonetheless true that there are some social obligations and forms of labor that, by their quality or by their quantity, are particularly inhuman. Yet the crushing and exploitation of the masses by a minority appears to have been the cruel and necessary condition of civilization's progress.[210] For Marxism-Leninism, unrestrained economic liberalism, as a factor in technical progress and of concentration and organization, was a necessary stage that prepared for the dawn of socialism.[211]

Most certainly, we now have at our disposal the technological means which, combined with a certain manner of using the general technological relation, may allow the forces of man to be less and less exhausted through the labor of animals or machines.[212] Should we, for all that, think that new elites will cease thriving on the grossly inhuman labor of others and thereby improving the humanity of all? Would they not also bear the stain of injustice and inhumanity?

For our part, in the same way that we prefer in ourselves the tendency towards universality, we would like it to be realized in each and every person, in equality and diversity, and we strive to draw the consequences from this preference and desire. This choice, is it necessary or not? Is it obligatory? Is it or is it not free in the second sense of the word liberty? All questions of beauty aside—the French style of gardening does not suit the taste of everyone—let us be satisfied to recall what we said about the innateness of the spirit of service in a number of species, as well as the Marxist opinion that changes in social superstructures in general and particularly in rights become inevitable when the relationships of production undergo a shift in balance.

Necessary or not, when once the choice has been made on the level of broad social options, another level of coherence through internal necessity appears on the level of secondary options. In the social domain as in others, morality involves a kind of geometry. The meaning of the postulates must always be weighed, along with the rigor of the explicitation; their dimensions must be gauged, and theory must always be confronted with practice. In the *Manifesto* of 1872, Marx and Engels speak of *"an association wherein the liberty of each is the condition of the liberty of all."* But some claim that in the Soviet Union there was a time when, under the pretext of the dictatorship of the proletariat, there was no longer a base of soviets, when a part of the intelligentsia was imprisoned in concentration camps or psychiatric clinics, when the most gross forms of persecution ran rampant, and not only against the remnants of past persecutions or against what could carry the seed of new persecutions . . . In his encyclical *Pacem in terris*, John XXIII similarly grounds himself on a natural definition of the liberty of universality without involving any religious belief. But at the same time that he recommends an admirable ordination of each to all and all to each within this perspective, he assigns as one of the inalienable rights of a human person that of private possession of the means of production, which some look upon as one of the surest routes toward slavery, and he implicitly introduces prescriptions rejected as inadequate and limiting by other free men, other Christian churches, and even by a number of Catholics. Without avoiding the necessity for certain disciplines within groups, we must take care that abstract explicitations, tutors, and frameworks of development, which are perhaps useful at certain times and in a certain way, do not end up by hindering our growth.

Combat, competition, mutual aid, accord and disaccord, reciprocal influences.

It is in combat, competition, mutual aid, accord and disaccord, reciprocal influence, in, through and for relation, that individuals, groups, civilizations, and species are born, differentiated, developed, conserved, changed, suffer regression or die.

"The struggle for existence among organized beings throughout the entire world must inevitably proceed from the geometrical progression of their numerical increase."[213] *"The progress of the average level of morality and the increase in number of individuals well gifted in this respect bestows a certain and immense advantage upon one tribe over another tribe. If one tribe comprises many members who possess a high degree of the spirit of patriotism, faithfulness, obedience, courage, and sympathy, who are consequently always prepared to sacrifice for the common good, it must clearly prevail over other tribes.*[214] Such are two points of view held by Darwin successively, twenty years apart, the second under the influence of Wallace. He placed emphasis on a certain complementarity between the combat and mutual aid and saw therein one of the two great factors in the evolution of species, the second being hereditary chance variation.

All black humor aside, like it or not, the prey, the victim, renders a service to the one who devours it. One of the most impressive examples of obligatory mutual consumption is the carbon cycle, in which one half of all living beings, that which is unable to accomplish photosynthesis, finds itself forced under pain of death to eat the other half. Modern ethology has made more precise descriptions of the modalities of combat, commensalism, and mutual aid between different species and within species. It reserves, perhaps somewhat abusively, the word aggression for an attack of one individual upon another individual belonging to the same species.[215] It shows that aggressive drives are combatted by contrary drives in each individual, and that this is observed in innate behaviors as well as in learned behaviors, the result being that combat within the group is attenuated and the group is preserved. Briefly, ethology, like psychoanalysis and human psychology, teaches us that what the living organism combats within itself and outside itself is frequently combat itself. This gives rise to varied forms of compromise, condensation, repression, conversion, displacement, transformation into the contrary, sublimation, symbolization, ritualization, and so on, that are equally observed in conflicts between other drives, and whose positive or negative consequences for individual development are often considerable. The gull that tears furiously at a bit of foliage rather than the feathers or the eyes of its neighbor, i.e., its ally and its antagonist, its friend and its enemy, its helper and its hinderer, is on the road that leads to other competitions, to the Olympic Games, to spiritual combats, to the most noble conquests . . . Whatever may be the relationships between combat and mutual aid, more or less consciously or unconsciously, voluntarily or involuntarily, each and all profit from the sacrifice of each, and at the same time each contributes towards his own self-realization through self-sacrifice for another.

As it plumbs, clarifies, and completes the views of classic psychology, psychoanalysis fundamentally studies the normal and pathological development of social relationships. It shows us the innate and learned drives that are more or less adapted, in part through the "ego," to each other and to social demands which are in conformity with reason or out of conformity with it. The authentic rationality of the ego passes through the sieve of free examination. It accepts, refuses, modifies, perfects . . . Some psychoanalysts fail to perceive this and, in flagrant contradiction to their own doctrine, reduce the ego to a tranquil and unconscious introjection of examples, silences, taboos, recommendations, injunctions, interdictions, chastisements, and rewards of the group, i.e., to the "super-ego." The latter contributes to the unconscious, to the scornful refusal of various biological drives, transforming them into the "id." The true ego enlightens the id and the super-ego. From somewhat different angles we have already noted all this; we will see it again in connection with the purgative way, the way of catharsis, disillusionment, of the awakening of consciousness and choice.

Psychoanalysis shows us how good and bad relational habits form in the infant within that miniature society called the family, or whatever takes its place, and how they undergo analogical repetition in later social relations, in positive or negative ways, frequently with extraordinary tenacity. It shows us a thrilling abridgement of the development of the person when, along with the modification of transference and the awakening of consciousness, old affective habits that have become inadequate, unrelated, and restricting, give place to freer behavior. It does not deny the existence of a sphere of development free of conflicts, [216] at least of present conflicts if we accept that except for chance mutations there is nothing in present life that is not a result of past combat. But it dwells on the multiplicity of conflicts, on their nature, their modes of resolution or nonresolution, and their predominant influence upon the development of the individual in relation and of the group. It teaches us how the overriding social attitudes of the adolescent and the adult result from the way in which early contradictions are resolved or fail to be resolved, how early battles are won or lost: the way in which others are looked upon, aggressiveness, fear, guilt, passive obedience, inferiority, defeat, isolation and other inadequate defense mechanisms, identification, contest, surmounting, and transcending, to name but a few.[217]

We have touched upon some types of human societies. There are societies which tend to promote a certain blossoming of some at the expense of others.

Others appear to claim a higher degree of reality than their members, forgetting that, if they do differ from the sum of their members, they also contain that sum, that, no matter how ephemeral it may be, consciousness does not exist outside the individual, and that a million times zero never amounts to more than zero. Still others are grounded on a mutual ordering of each to all and all to each, on the awareness and presentiment of humanity in potency within each man and on the willingness to assist in the development of each and all in unity and diversity, taking into account material foundations and necessary steps.[218] We have stated where our preferences lie. They are, it seems, no more than a drop of water in the sea, yet animated by the movement of the sea, an individual expression of the deep logic of things.

7   *Disillusionment, the Awakening of Consciousness, and Choice*

Motivations. Necessity of choosing, liberty or necessity in choice, and the choice of liberty.

We have noted numerous affective tendencies within man in society. As the realization of these tendencies goes on, the finality of pleasure is often, but not always, found to be in accord with other advantages for the individual, group, or species. The majority of these tendencies already exists at prior biological levels. Heredity delivers them partly prepared and partly unexercised, subjected to relations, conciliation, contest; and here occurs one of the first functions of learning and intelligence. Soon intellectual activity detaches itself in part from basic needs and finds a new source of satisfaction, pleasure, and happiness in the discovery of the world. Both our reason in its two functions and our more primitive functions are consonant with the principle of originality and reciprocal adaptation, that is, in a sense, with different degrees and modalities of logic and truth. These are all taken into consideration when it is said, and justly so, that we are moved by "love of the truth." First and foremost, to be is to be in a true relation.

But experience teaches us that we are also moved by the "love of beauty." This notion is no less complex than the preceding. Aesthetic feeling can correspond to sublimations, symbolizations, stylizations, other transformations of the majority of our instincts, to the order, repetitions and rhythms of the real, to conservation and novelty, to the satisfaction linked to reciprocal adaptation. Reflect, if you will, on the diversity of emotions and pleasures aroused in us by the works of a Wagner, a Beethoven, or a J. S. Bach, on the beauty found in a gothic cathedral[219] or a Parthenon, in a face, a voice, a nude, a countryside, one's homeland . . . Here once again, we doubtlessly can observe roots in the evolution of living beings, like sexual dress and ostentation, stylized gestures, certain nest decorations, or the dog I saw on several occasions peacefully sitting on a wall, indifferent to passersby, looking, it seemed to me, at the sunset over the ocean.

Conflicts, compositions, exclusions, transformations of innate or learned drives, of unconscious introjections from the group, and the orderings towards increased pleasure or decreased displeasure, towards other individual, social, and specific forms of utility: this dialectic of affectivity, not entirely devoid of logic and truth, does not require a high degree of consciousness and reason. In different degrees and modalities these are observable among our lesser brothers, small children, and the most simple-minded of men. When the highest rationality takes a hand in the search for happiness, contributing towards the old satisfactions, and adding to them its own pleasures, it enters into the combat from which it has probably arisen; in its turn it must order, create hierarchy, compose, transform, exclude . . . In this activity man emerges as neither beast nor angel; he does not despise the old instincts; he is able to satisfy them in a suitable way, taking for his rule not to be blinded or ensnared by the part, so as to keep himself free in respect to the whole. Once again, this is a simple fact of observation. In this supreme choice, however, as much as in partial choices more or less ordered towards it, one question continues to stand out: are we free to make ourselves free or to refuse to be free?

To choose means to commit oneself and set out along one path and not upon another. To say that choice is necessary is simply to say that we cannot develop in two different directions, along two different courses, at the same time. It is another way of formulating the principle of identity, whether "deinstantized" or not, considered from the angle of ancient formal logic or from the angle of dialectic that embraces the first without annihilating it. It is also a declaration of the immutability of the past, of a certain impossibility of dedifferentiation, of a certain irreversibility of time. The choice of liberty constitutes one particular case: the interest in the whole is correlative with a certain detachment vis-à-vis the part.

More or less explicitly, to a greater or lesser degree, liberty is effectively chosen by the majority of men. Any naturalist can observe that. Zoologically speaking, it is this very thing that serves to define our species. For one who is able to recognize the identity of deeply rooted attitudes under differences of language, this choice appears in the most diverse theoretical frameworks as well as in their absence, even in the case of the person who chooses to live without too much reflection, without too much preoccupation about *Weltanschauung,* truth, logic, and internal coherence, to be led about by men and events. By definition the least act of reason contains an element of universality, and therefore a little liberty. Nevertheless, liberty can be more or less reduced and more or less obscured by contrary tendencies.

One must choose. As for knowing whether we are forced to choose this over that, or whether in this choice we are free in the second sense of the word, this is, as we have also seen, an entirely different question. It can be posed, or appear to be posed, in reference to three degrees or modalities of choice with no change whatsoever in respect to facts: the general choice of the liberty of universality or its refusal; partial choices in or out of line with a greater liberty of movement within the whole, either favoring it or not (and in this sense the liberty of choice and the choice of liberty become one); choices, if there be any, indifferent to the preceeding point of view. For a certain number of theologians and philosophers, the attraction exerted by the totality would be stronger than the force of the part; the theoretical difficulty would not be in "superdetermination" by the first but in determination by the second when it runs contrary to the former. They put forward, as characteristic of our free will, a power to refuse the totality. We have wondered, in respect to the psychological analysis they give of this power of refusal, whether they have effected a pure and simple displacement of the problem: from "action" to "thought," from both to the "focus of attention," and ending up finally back again at the critique of the notion of potentiality.[220]

For our part, we are still limiting ourselves to setting forth a fact of observation (further verifying a logical necessity): the correlation existing between suppression of intellectual and affective encumbrance, detachment from obstructing illusions, and the increase within us of the liberty of universality.

Actuality, inactuality, insufficiencies and excesses of the Cartesian project.

The "Discourse of Method" is profoundly human. It is initially an affirmation of the preeminence of the reasonable ego over the unconscious introjections, fallaciously or validly rationalized, of the injunctions of the group, over what the psychoanalysts have subsequently called the superego. This is not to say that the drives of the id, their obscure inner conflicts and those with social agencies, are not also foreseen by Descartes as capable of constituting a factor of illusion: *"Since we have all been children before becoming men, and for a long time obliged to be governed by our appetites and our teachers, the two of which often contradicting each other and unenlightened in their counsels . . ."*[221] Nor is this to say that our former conduct should be systematically rejected, especially if it is in conformity with that of the other members of the group, avoids extremes, and does not compromise our quest: it is given the benefit of the doubt and held in virtue of a provisional moral code until submitted to reason's examination. The more moderate it is, the easier it will be for us to modify it if reason so ordains: a remark which leads us to believe that Descartes had not yet seen contrary arise from contrary . . . Finally, the senses and the sensory imagination themselves are looked upon as doubtful, and the existence of that which seems different from our own thinking, like and even prior to everything else, requires demonstration. It is in respect to this last point, as we have said, that we differ from Descartes.

Descartes found in the *cogito* the only solid evidence, the only possible proof of the existence of God and of the world. In this we see above all an affirmation and a choice of a propensity, the propensity towards being, through thought. Implicitly, and even explicitly, Descartes had already discovered this tendency within himself, and had chosen it in his choice to be a seeker and not to assign this choice the character of a provisional morality. Or, if you prefer, the justification for the quest was clearly, for Descartes, more immediately coessential with the *cogito* than what he derived from it as first logical consequences. To detect within himself a kind of flight and to fear and refuse every form of containment seem to have been for him one single movement.

Provisional or not, based on internal logic or prudence, opportunity, egoism, lack of class consciousness, social realism, or for whatever other motive, the morality of the *Discourse* is, in one respect, individualistic and aristocratic: *"The single resolve to divest oneself of all past beliefs is not one that should be taken by all men. The world is mostly divided into two sorts of men, for neither of which would this be a good decision . . . ";* among these Descartes disregarded, or pretended to do so, those whose humble and exhausting work allowed him his own laborious leisure. Perhaps other forms of the division of labor were inconceivable at that time. But among these he does include *"those who, having sufficient reason or modesty to decide that they are less capable than some others in distinguishing between truth and falsehood and that these may be their instructors, ought rather to be satisfied to follow the opinions of these others than to seek out better ones by themselves."* Thus Descartes seems to feel that what is required of most is to abandon their reason to certain individuals, and this is in odd contrast with his affirmation that *"good sense is the most well shared commodity in the world."* Added to his reassurances concerning his civic mindedness and his faith, as well as to the social, political, and religious mores of his day, this contradiction in language leaves room for doubt that Descartes was being more than ironical here, deploring the state of things, and hoping. Galileo had just been summoned to retract and did so without hesitation knowing that things are what they are, that sooner or later truth would blaze forth, and no more aware than his inquisitors that his system would one day be engulfed into a system more vast.

Nevertheless, while the initial stages of his life plan were providing its author with the happiness inherent in personal development,[222] and no matter what we might think of his possible acceptance, conscious or unconscious, or of his veiled refusal of the material and spiritual oppression of others, Descartes's project is clearly impregnated by the spirit of service, the desire for the common good, and the will to teamwork. Nor does he neglect the earth in favor of Heaven: *". . . but as soon as I had acquired some general notions about physics, and when I started to test them in various particular difficulties, I saw where they could lead and how they differed from the principles which had been invoked up to the present time, and I believed that I could not keep them hidden without sinning grievously against the law that obliges us to procure, as far as we are able, the general good of all men. For they led me to see that it is possible to arrive at knowledge that is highly useful in life, and that. . . we can make ourselves like the masters and possessors of Nature. And this is desirable not only for the discovery of an infinity of artifices by which we may painlessly enjoy the fruits of the earth and all its comforts, but more especially for the preservation of health, which is without a doubt the principal and most basic among all the goods of this life; for the spirit is so dependent upon the temperament and disposition of the bodily organs, that, if it is possible to find a means by which men in general can be rendered wiser and more capable than hitherto, I believe it is in medicine that it should be sought. . . all that is known about it is practically nothing in comparison with what remains to be known, and we can free ourselves from an infinity of illnesses, corporal as much as spiritual, and perhaps even from the debilitation of old age . . . But, when I had decided to devote my entire life to seeking out such a necessary science and had come across a way which seemed to me such as to lead to it without fail, there remained two obstacles to surmount: the shortness of life and the lack of experience. I made the decision that the best remedy against these two obstacles was to communicate faithfully to the public all the little I myself should have found and to incite those of superior spirit to go further, each contributing according to his inclination and possibilities to the required experiments, communicating faithfuly to the public all that they should learn in order that the last might begin where the former left off. In this way, joining together the lives and labors of many, we might together go much further than each in particular by himself could do."* One could hardly add that, for a Christian, Descartes did not seem at all in a hurry to arrive at Heaven, and that, for a dualist of correspondence if not of outright separation, he saw the psychosomatic medicine of the future attribute a preeminence to the corporeal aspect and approach. At the same time he codified a cathartic method essentially oriented toward science, but not without relationships with spirituality, and the psychoanalysis of the future. As for transformations of social structures, despite all the reservations we have proposed, he was not without some awareness of their possibility, perhaps even their necessity and the violence involved: *"It is too difficult to rebuild these large bodies once they have been beaten down, or even to maintain them once shaken, and their collapse can only be dreadful."*

Correlation between disillusionment and the awakening of consciousness.

"What is true on this side of the Pyrenees is an error beyond them." It is, Descartes tells us, the variability and contradiction of human opinions according to locations, times, societies, systems, age, food, digestion, wakefulness, or sleep, the fact of having had several teachers instead of only one, of having traveled the world and enjoyed solitude, of having listened to others and to himself, that awakened him to the methodic doubt and to free examination. From the clash of contrary doctrines, from the ensuing emptiness and darkness, from the interior silence there arose an affirmation and choice of a tendency. In order to persist in its process of realization this tendency had to continue to use the method which led to its rising into consciousness: in relationship, confrontation, and isolation, to let the false make room for the true, and the true replace the false.

Clearly, styles of spirituality are not all the same. There are differences, regressions, improvements. There are obstacles and snares, and who can boast of having avoided or surmounted all of them? Perhaps, along with St. Benedict, western monastic spirituality had left Descartes wary of too much isolation. Perhaps the fact of having been formed for a long time within a community, under a rule and an abbot, before devoting himself to eremetical solitary meditation, may have prevented him from mistaking dreams for reality, or at least from having the fear of doing so . . .[223] Modern socialism, for its part, has no more disdain for man. For it, however, there is no question in human relations of being, as Descartes put it, a spectator rather than an actor: spiritual progress takes place through technique, practice, commitment, team work, class consciousness, and social combat. Human sciences have taught us much about ourselves. We better understand our own growth. Analytical catharsis is correlative with the awakening of consciousness: here again that which could have been true at some other time, but has become false, is exposed and set aside to make room for true relations. Group activity, autocritic or heterocritic, fraternal correction, brain washing, are increasingly correlative with the liberty of information. Education and instruction tend increasingly, through increasingly more appropriate means, towards "the liberty of each as a condition of the liberty of all,"[224] and less and less towards propaganda. Descartes would have rejoiced at this.

In addition to the preceding considerations, may I be permitted a personal observation? In this dialectic of disillusionment and awakening of consciousness, of the old and the new, the true and the false, of reciprocal emptying, the contradictory relation, the conflict, and the solitude are sometimes initially imposed in an extremely violent and grossly exterior way. When I was a young man, at once full of an ambitious project and all manner of old, stereotyped views, neither understanding the meaning of the one nor being aware of the others, knowing less than nothing about myself and the world, I had no inkling that life would soon force me to take other voyages and make other confrontations than those for which I was preparing myself to be a physician in the French Navy. First there were my encounters with travelers, the war, and solitude, and what encounters they were! However my lot was less cruel than that of others. Instead of being crushed I was invigorated, and there arose a zest for disillusionment and the awakening of consciousness. The correlation between these and their continuation within relation and solitude, through concrete experience, information and meditation, appeared to me more and more as one of the modalities and conditions of my own development and of such services as, at least hopefully, I would render to others. Later didactic psychoanalysis helped shed even greater light on myself and enabled me to understand my fellow men better. Continuing the *catharsis* is not without difficulties, effort, and struggle; it is called availability and openness as well as reexamination. Catharsis does not exclude necessary conservations from the awakening of consciousness, nor that margin of uncertainty or of extrapolation which so often distinguishes practice, and even fundamental choices, from the certainty of science, but does prevent the old from preventing the new within us, even at the cost of harrowing revisions.

At the same time that he consecrated his life to inquiry, Descartes decided that inquiry was coessential with his being: between *est* and *non,* i.e., between being and nonbeing, he chose to be, and for him and in him being was fundamentally connoted by consciousness, and the growth of being by that of consciousness. He observed in man tendencies such as the spirit of service, to say nothing of the love of neighbor, or the tendency to delegate reason and to blind obedience. If he did not declare that to be is to love,[225] to serve, or to obey without understanding, he did love, serve, and either judged or pretended to judge that it could be good to abandon one's judgment to another. Three centuries later we were to hear an intelligent Chinese declare that he desired with all his strength to become a tiny wheel in an immense machine, that to be was, in sum, not to think, and that, by way of consequence, our duty was to diminish consciousness within ourselves and within others, with no consequent collective increase in all men. But we have strong reasons to think that this was simply a refined expression of humor. As for us, our view is that our reasoning species is not destined for extinction, at least not for a long time. Clearly, here again concrete truth is synthetic, and the tendency of each and all towards universality is undoubtedly more characteristic of the concrete individual in concrete relationships than an ego affirming itself in a vainglorious and absurd isolation, or humbly and no less absurdly annihilated in the group. This double affirmation seems rooted deep within the world of the living, and still more generally in the whole of reality.

Saint Philbert de Grand Lieu,
April 1972

Part Four

Economic and Cultural Problems

Production, consumption and human development.
Our intelligence is in part oriented towards fabrication. At the same time, under certain conditions, fabrication continues to develop us through the goods of civilization that it places at our disposal, by the clarifying confrontation between "praxis" and reality, by the self-discipline, the pleasure of discovery, making, serving, team work, the sense of functional beauty provided by the object . . . all experienced in the process of fabrication itself. But there is a contradiction to overcome from the outset: time is needed to fabricate the goods of civilization, and time is needed to enjoy them.

Time, said Marx, is the field of our development. Indeed, it connotes change, our own as well as that of the clock. For many of us, time is subdivided into work time and leisure time. This does not necessarily mean time of activity and time of unemployment or sleep. It means as well time for harder work, work that is more forced, more directed, more fragmentary, more oriented towards the production of elementary goods and services, and time for more spontaneous activities, susceptible of a higher degree of personal humanization and not necessarily devoid of the broadest social value.

To study the relations between economy and culture, the latter in the sense of personal development, is to study the quantitative and qualitative evolution of the times of basic work and leisure activities, of the goods and services produced and of the social division of labor, product and time.

1   *Quantitative and Qualitative Level of Employ-ment in Its Relations with Automation, Production, Con-sumption, Expansion and Demography, in Different Eco-nomic Systems. General Technological Relation*

Automatic production.

By definition productivity increases to the extent that the same quantity of the same goods and services requires a lesser quantity of human labor. The increase of productivity can be achieved by widely varying means, from the organization of labor and mechanization to a change in the product, as long as the latter's class of use remains the same. Automation is a particular class of productivity. The quantity of human labor is in direct relation with the extent of production and in inverse relation with that of automation. When automation is increased in a limited industrial sector, to an equal quantity of human labor and an increased quantity of product in that sector, there corresponds a quantity of human labor that is more pronounced in the areas of input and output to the extent that automation is lacking in these areas. Not only does the quantity of labor vary with automation, but also its quality. The same can apply to goods and services produced, with the preservation of previous classes of usage and with the possibility of new uses.

In a competitive system motivated by profit,[226] [227] the latter (technological differential or marginal profit) arises, among other ways, from the difference of the cost of the product manufactured respectively in a technically advanced enterprise, with high productivity and mass production,[228] including less human labor in the final production cycle, and other enterprises. The differential technological profit increases in importance to the degree that two other forms of profit linked, at least according to Marxist analysis,[229] with nonremunerated surplus labor (absolute excess value and relative excess value) are hampered by the workers' progress in self-defense. It fosters technical progress, because enterprises that are less advanced in productivity, in automation, must align themselves for survival with the most advanced, and the latter must maintain the difference. It has a double effect on the quantity of human labor in two opposite directions: the labor increases with the increase in production (itself facilitated by that of productivity and in relation to the need for increasing the absolute quantity of profit when the benefit margin tends to diminish)[230] but decreases with the increase in productivity and automation.

In a system that is monopolistic or based upon agreement, if the means of production and the product remain private property, and profit an important motive, market prices can be exaggerated.[231] This can be accompanied by product scarcity with a consequent diminution of human labor more than proportional to a possible increase in automation. When this process involves goods of general use without increase in salaries, it can increase social injustice. When the face value of salaries increases in proportion to the rising cost of living (salary index), like differential technological profit in a competitive system, the differential or marginal profit can still bring about a surge forward, but now it is designed to conserve a gap between sale prices and costs (the corresponding increase in salaries experiences a certain lag), and not to maintain an advance in technology. It is conceivable that this can constitute an inflationary factor.[232] In any case it can result in another stagnation in technology.

In a strongly directed collectivist monopoly the importance of profit can be considered as less, and the level of production, productivity, and employment can be decided, at least in theory, by central authority in function of other criteria.

In the case of abundant manpower, full employment with its human significance (right to work), political significance (social peace), and economic significance (the ability to buy what industry produces), can imply extensive expansion, i.e., an increase in the capacity for production and in effective production without any increase in automation. Let us recall, however, that an increase in automation within a limited, well chosen sector of industry, can, by increasing the intensity of production on the level of that sector, increase the quantity of human labor within both the input and output sectors to the extent that they are less automated. As for the necessary infrastructure (basic knowledge, communications, etc. . .), the example of different countries that were underdeveloped until quite recently and then within a few decades came to enjoy an astounding transfer of technology, shows that, given certain conditions, it can take shape rapidly. There is general agreement that this requires detailed planning as a minimum.[233]

All else being equal, automation tends to reduce the quantitative level of employment, if not on the level of global economy at least in the sector involved. It frequently necessitates continuous production, hence night-work. The quality of work changes. So far two principal changes have been observed: workers less and less qualified, focused more and more on fragmentary aspects of jobs, common workers of automation, hardly more than appendages of machines; technicians and engineers who are highly qualified, but in a sense no less specialized. As for the repercussions of automation in one sector on the quantity and quality of work on the level of sectors dealing with the input and output, these depend equally on the level and modalities of their automation.

Among the retroactive consequences of one sector's automation on input sectors are the production of automatons and of men qualified to use them; consequently, among other things advanced technological research and basic technological teaching; this is the sense in which the latter constitutes a part of the infrastructure when technology is introduced to a nation in process of development. But it is not certain that the discovery and use of IBM equipment necessarily involves a great human culture, especially when the emphasis is placed more on profitability, which, for cost effectiveness, tends to reduce the formation of workers on all levels to a strict minimum. But this observation does not slight in the least the value of automatons; they can have a profound human significance, and not just in the highly efficient manufacture of elementary goods and services . . .[234]

We feel that automation can constitute an element of liberation, but under certain conditions. The first, it seems, would be that its effects on the quantita-tive reduction of human labor should not be wiped out by an ill proportioned increase in total production, as happens, for example, in the case of exaggerated, unbridled production, consumption, and expansion. The second and third conditions would be an *ad hoc* demography and distribution. Why, then, should a kind of civil work service not oblige each of us to devote a small part of our time to field, forest, and factory? As for the remainder of our time, there would probably be a relationship between the way it would be used and the usefulness of the goods and services produced by the preceding modalities of labor, even though they are still quite elementary, and at the same time, through our leisure activities, other goods and other services could be discovered, produced, and owned.

It may also be expected that the major obstacle to a terrestrial paradise of self-conceived, self-manufactured, self-controlled, and self-repaired auto-matons, to the free harvest from automatic distributors, will perhaps not be technical, nor even economic. To the union member wondering who might buy the goods and services, and in exchange for what, if most of them were no longer manufactured by human workers, perhaps Henry Ford would have replied that the economy of free harvest is in correlation to the disappearance of exchange, of exchange value, and of the various forms of industrial ownership. He would have so added these strange bedfellows to other indices that Ricardo's principle of the work value would perhaps not be so obsolete as various economists maintain. The true difficulty will be rather in our vocation as expanding microcosms, in our taste for another fruit, that of the tree of knowledge and power. This will continue to demand work, and not just the work of a machine. . .

Consumption.

Consumption is the name given to the use of goods and services regardless of whether or not this use is accompanied by attrition. Individual consumption is only a part of it. The quantitative level of employment, inversely related to automation, is in direct relation to production, and therefore to consumption. The former constitutes the upper limit of the latter, and the two have a mutually stimulating effect on each other.

An economy that tends towards profit naturally sets production according to demand (individual, collective, or otherwise) at the same time that it tends to increase demand quantitatively and to direct it qualitatively in the direction of profit: *"marketing"* has a double meaning.[235] An abundance of individual and collective goods is not excluded; quite the reverse is true. But several problems remain in addition to the tendency towards unchecked production, consumption and expansion, among which is the question of the human value of the goods and services produced, and that of their distribution.

In a strongly controlled collectivist system central authority, which is thought to seek the common good and to motivate the economy in its interests, is clearly less committed to foster consumption. It can see to the satisfaction of the needs of the collectivity as such before that of individual needs. This does not exclude great strides forward in the planned production of goods for collective and even individual consumption (the suppression of famines, the promotion of literacy, health, basic education, infrastructure, primary industries, advanced technology, atomic energy, space, etc. . .)[236] Profit can persist as a means to this end (plan accountability, the self-financing of enterprises, fictitious competition, etc.). Increased production tends to increase the quantitative level of employment, so much the more as the degree of automation is initially weaker (extensive expansion).[237] However there do seem to be certain limits as to how much the worker may be burdened with an overwhelming quantity or inhuman quality of labor: from this point of view it is instructive to compare the epoch of Smith and Dickens in England to Soviet Russia[238] and modern China . . . To tell the truth, the two latter countries, particularly China, have had the benefits of a transfer of technology.

From the beginnings of industrialization, the buying power of the masses has, as a whole, increased in developed countries. Whether the cause of this be the lowering of costs of goods and services along with an increase in productivity and mass production, unionization, the change-over from private to collective property, or the combination of these various factors plus others in varying proportions and manners, the fact seems undeniable. One of the best indicators of this is clearly the qualitative change in family budgets, in which the part set aside for the purchase of primary goods has progressively decreased. Nevertheless, there continue to be relative inequalities, sometimes of a shocking degree, as much within various developed countries as between developed and underdeveloped countries, and a manifest lack in absolute value. There are still millions of unemployed. Two thirds of the inhabitants of the planet are still simply undernourished while, of the remaining third, some goods of civilization, such as higher education, have only begun to spread. As far as the world is concerned, there is a great void that remains to be filled before the problem of unrestrained consumption and its various correlations with our use of time can be addressed in all of its breadth.

Expansion.

Expansion or growth is the increase in prcduction calculated materially or in value, whether in a direct or indirect way (output measured either materially or, combined with profit, in value, assuming the manufacturing process to be at capacity in both cases, and furthermore, in the second, the value of money to be constant). The increase in industrial capital, i.e., investments in stock and equipment, constitutes a part of it and is deducted from profit; it is subject to depreciation along with wear and tear. All else being equal on the side of productivity in general and automation in particular, real expansion (i.e., measuring the increase in concrete production, and not the diminution in value of money) is in direct relation to the increase in the quantity of human labor. If for no other reason than the fact that an increase in production very frequently accompanies an increase in productivity, i.e., a dimuntion in the human labor expended during the final cycle of production per unit of product, the value of production can increase less rapidly than its concrete quantity. It can even decrease while the latter increases.[239] Consumption, in the broad sense, is the goal of production. The latter is the upper limit of the former. Concrete production and consumption vary in the same direction, and while they are on the increase they tend to increase the quantity of employment, which automation tends to decrease. Overproduction, or production without consumption, constitutes a supplementary, artificial factor in the increase of work.

When we consider an Adam Smith market, i.e., a competitive market with profit as the principal motivator, the requirements of both factors push inexorably towards the increase of production and productivity. This is the life blood of the system, consisting in invested capital, or, more exactly, in the part of profit leading to capitalization, focusing on the points of greatest growth. There are risks to be faced by exaggerated production, consumption, and expansion, and possibly by deregulation and overproduction. But without even mentioning some of the more human consequences of unbridled expansion in general, we have seen that Adam Smith's marginalist rush towards productivity, towards automation, is a powerful factor in technical progress.

Concentration.

The lowering of costs, the increase in production and productivity, and product marketing, all require an ever greater concentration of industrial capital.[240] Marx saw in this one of the greatest positive contributions of private capital, which began the socialization of production, and, through a progressive disequilibrium of the forces facing each other, prepared for the change from private industrial ownership to collective ownership; perhaps he underestimated a little the possibilities of automation, unions, high salaries, small stockholdings, and the regulatory influences of the State. Three quarters of a century later Lenin observed that the process had expanded and, calling it "economic imperialism," he interpreted it in the same way as had Marx.[241] We had best recognize that, on the whole, concentration has continued to increase.[242]

Thus contrary springs dialectically from contrary, from competition comes concentration, and from struggle comes the absence of struggle. In a private monopoly or oligopoly, competition diminishes. If the maximum increase of profit is no longer quite so vital, profit nevertheless remains an

important objective.[243] Adam Smith's rush towards production and pro-
ductivitiy, an element in technical progress and, in a certain way, of
abundance, involves the risk of being replaced by technical stagnation,
rising prices and, if salaries follow, of inflation.[244] If they do not follow,
then there is the risk of creating scarcity and social injustice.

Whether it results from the collective appropriation of a private monopoly
or in some other fashion, collective monopoly involves a high degree of
concentration, organization, and hierarchical structure. Perhaps more so
than in private monopolistic or oligopolistic systems, centrifugal influences
tend to predominate. Central authority looks to the collective good, the good
of the individual, and the relations between them, and it plans production
with these in mind without being committed to survey demand and to solicit
it for profit.[245] Economic clashes have vanished, which is quite amazing for
an ideology which makes of struggle the moving force of change. Fear has
been expressed that out of this can grow a disproportion between goods
consumed by the individual and certain collective goods, as well as stagnation of technology in certain sectors of production (extensive expansion with
weak productivity). Some have gone so far as to advocate the reestablishment of a certain competition within the limits of the general plan, thereby
allowing contrary once again to arise from contrary, or at least allowing
them to coexist.[246] [247] Others have thought it preferable to bolster and perfect
still more the central directorate without thereby excluding the motivations,
initiative,and responsibility of the periphery, and centripetal information.
This would be one of the profound meanings of the recent events at Prague
and Brezhnev's report on the economy, followed by an increase in concentration, hierarchical structure, planning and division of labor within Com-
econ.

In a tempered capitalist system, governments are torn between two
contrary tendencies: the favoring of a certain degree of concentration and the
maintaining of a certain degree of competition. Along with conjunctural
politics and progressive taxation, antitrust laws constitute one of the aspects
of moderate state intervention. The opposition of governments to extreme
forms of the tendency towards concentration of private industrial capital
seems to indicate that the state does not coincide entirely with the interests of
the latter and that, on this point, politics perhaps loses something of its
characterization as a simple reflection of economics: the reason for this
clearly lies in a certain effectiveness of universal suffrage, political parties,
unions, special interest groups, lobbies, pressure groups, etc. . . .[248] [249]

Whether motivated by profit, the common good, or by both at once, whether they are unrestricted, planned, partially planned, or simply controlled, whatever may be the priorities and the interactions, the perspectives that are possible for consumption, production, and expansion are probably limitless in a certain respect. They are in the closest possible rapport with the knowledge, conquest, possession, and transformation of the exterior world and of ourselves, increased without limit in depth and breadth. Some are alarmed by the exponential character of growth. Others maintain that our only limit would be a law of the final equalization of energy, to say nothing of the fact that, after all, we are not God . . .

General technological relation.

Along with S. A. D. Bukhari and F. & J. Morette, we have come to feel that one part of the preceding considerations can be summed up in a very simple formula: *the quantity of labor required from man is in direct relation to concrete consumption, production and expansion, and in inverse relation to automation. In the case of automation of a limited sector, the variation of the quantity of human labor at the input and output sectors is in direct relation to the variation in the quantity of production at the level of the automated sector, and in inverse relation to the degree of automatization at the input and output sectors. The multiplier of employment can be larger or smaller than the unit, or equal to it. Increase in production can take place extensively at any sector, with an increase in human labor and without an increase in productivity. But in general automation can further increase the output of production.*[250] Exaggerated consumption, production, and unrestricted expansion lead to an increase in employment, while automation leads to a reduction. The quality of elementary work and leisure activities is in relation to the quantity and quality of the goods and services produced and consumed. The general technological relation is nothing else than an explanation of the notion of productivity in the particular case of automation. In a sense it is a truism. The other ways of increasing productivity (rationalizing work, increasing production, etc.) are subsumed under the same relation.[251]

Demography.

These considerations must further take into account the quantitative relation between the part of the population bound to elementary labor and the total population. Indeed, the active part of the population, active in the sense just described, produces for total consumption. This ratio tends to decrease as a result of various factors such as an increase in the length of studies, a shortening of the work year, and a reduction of the number of years devoted to working. Until now increase in longevity has led to an increase in total population with a relative reduction of the active portion. On top of this must also be added the problem of the total distribution of labor, of the product, and of time. We will be returning to this.

A note regarding mathematical and experimental methods in economics.
Most of the time logico-mathematical analysis consults experience, both on the level of premises and that of verification. It is necessarily abstract. As long as it is handled by man alone it requires broad simplifications, such as the equalization of all factors but one. One of the merits of Keynes' approach is that it has reminded us that concrete reality is complex, and that certain factors can be erroneously subsumed under the rubric "all else being equal" when they are dependent upon the variable under study. Thus the buying power of the masses may once have been reduced to increasing profits through cost reduction, in disregard of the fact that buyers are needed to make sales.[252]

The essential object of marginal analysis is not the attempt to hide certain profit mechanisms. It is to classic economic analysis what algebra is to arithmetic, or the study of one function in its continuity to that of the defined values of the function for defined values of the variable. The study of the slope or derivative of curves is conceived to be of great interest when there is question of differences, as in differential technological profit or in differential price/salary profit.

Computers enable logico-mathematical analysis to approach the complexity of concrete economics. The multiplicity of factors and of their interrelationships involves a lesser obstacle. At the present time, by means of these machines one aims at foreseeing the evolution of economic models under various hypotheses.

Quantitative and qualitative level of employment in its relationships to individual development.
Ontogeny, modern biology teaches us, depends at least on hereditary virtualities acquired and preserved throughout the course of the evolution of

species, as well as on the milieu and the exterior circumstances in which the individual develops. But a number of so-called genetic limitations are perhaps simply our present lack of ability to act upon growth. We already know how to predict, attenuate, or cure certain hereditary deficiencies. We know how to protect ourselves against certain subsequent aggressions from the milieu or to handle their consequences. We know how to prolong life, how to remove and transplant organs, install prostheses, and absorb techniques. The attainments of civilization are on the increase. The sciences of education are making progress. Instruction broadens its scope. Nevertheless, we are no more aware of the limits of individual virtualities than of the future of the species, nor even if there are limits other than ontological, as circumstances change. Perhaps the future progress of our means of affecting our own development is limitless. At any rate, what is presently at our disposal is clearly inferior to what will be, and it is certainly distributed with no regard for generosity or equality. For underdeveloped countries, the principal problem remains that of the employment and sustenance of the masses. As for developed countries, or those that are so called, the major part of their population is still relatively uneducated, and neuroses are an illness of the rich . . . or more exactly an illness from which only the rich can hope to be cured.

The quality of employment can be limited by a level of individual development independent of it: e.g., the use of mental deficients as industrial laborers. Huxley himself spoke bluntly of the *production* of cretins for the needs of industry.[253] The quality of employment and the crushing effect of its quantity can hinder development and can even provoke regressions. The forced transformation of men into kinds of machine appendices, whether teleguided or not, will doubtless be one of the great paradoxes of the twentieth century. In contrast, a certain quality of work, scheduled with moderation, can contribute to the development of the workingman.

Smithian hunger and profit. Levels of motivations.
In Smith's system both the product market and the labor market are perfectly competitive. If the supply of labor exceeds the demand for it, salaries can be maintained at what is required for bare subsistence. The worker should work to live in the most elementary sense of the word: "he who would not work, let him not eat" (if he belongs to the working class). This does not necessarily exclude pleasure associated with manufacture, as long as the task is not too isolated and is not without a sense of contributing to a project that benefits not only stock-holders but the public as well.

As for Smith's entrepreneur, he is unmotivated by elementary need: indeed, nothing prevents him from running through his capital if the stakes are insufficient. Classic analysis shows that, even if he does not wish to do so, Smith's entrepreneur is obliged to make the most of profit and to invest in industrial goods as much as possible, in such a way that he increases production and productivity, reduces costs and increases aptitude for competition and profit; which, in turn, starts the same process all over again.[254] This is the reason why Marx observed that his principal virtue lay not in his propensity towards consumption but in his inclination to save for the purpose of investment.[255] He was so bound by the imperatives of the system. The system, however, must be attractive enough for him to agree to be and remain involved in it. But if we exclude elementary biological motives and (at least as a dominant element, and with Keynes' reservations as to the necessity of consuming luxury items if it is felt that they should continue to be made) the propensity to use benefits first for luxury living, what psychological attractions does the system present?

Marx attributed the propensity of Smith's capitalism for profit and investment saving to the will towards power. *"The desire to dominate is one of the moving forces of the 'auri sacra fames,' "* and he cites Luther: *"He wishes to be the God of all [. . .] he would have all, all to himself, in order that each should receive from him as from a god and remain his serf forever."* Luther, to tell the truth, was still unaware of all but the most primitive forms of capital; he confused usury with hoarding up treasure; he had no awareness that Anglo-Saxon protestantism, followed with more or less assurance by Catholics and others, was going to plunder the Jews of one of the rare things that had not been taken from them, interest on loans, and thus to open the road to world conquest through the assistance of capital, or at least to allow it to happen, or to be unable to prevent it.

Comparative ethology shows us some of the distant origins of the will to power, domination, territory, substitution, displacement, sublimation, etc. . . Power, hierarchy, and even intellectual, spiritual, and "charitable" territories sometimes take still extremely archaic shapes: "do not search in my domain, do not teach my sheep or care for my poor;" the animal who marks off its territory or signalizes its power or its place in a hierarchy is acting in the same way. The owner of a territory will perhaps never exploit nor use more than a tiny fraction of it, but that does not prevent prohibition to trespass; this notion of differed or simply possible use, enjoyment, is already present among our lesser brothers. Scrooge's transformation[256] demonstrates a relative sublimation of the will to power into acts of beneficence; many, however, reject this kind of gift, feeling that the left hand gives back only a small part of what the right hand takes. Some psychoanalysts, moreover, have claimed to detect some analogies between hoarding and constipation, between the affirmation of potency and phallic exhibitionism and identification with one's father. To "eat into capital" or, having elected to remain in the system, to stop following its economic imperatives, these not only would invite the reprobation of the group, but even involve a risk of set-back and social impotence, not without analogy to castration: that of finding oneself "beyond the pale." Is it not one of the most archaic defenses against weakness to believe that one is omnipotent?

Be that as it may, more than the propensity to consume, Smith's imperative towards maximum profit appears initially reducible to that of saving for investment purposes and bringing the latter in line with the will to power. Nevertheless, experience teaches us that Smith's entrepreneur is no stranger to the consumption of luxury items, whether this is motivated by the needs of production, those of display, or by simple pleasure. Lastly, the satisfaction of the need to dominate, command, and organize, in company with an increased individual consumption, both diversified and seasoned with occasional acts of beneficence, can grow even further—the fact is hard to deny—with the pleasure of producing useful goods and services, even functional beauty, and of contributing to the general prosperity. From the viewpoint of comparative ethology this could correspond to the mutual assistance found within a species, or to aesthetic sensibility.

Subsequent modifications.

The workers' market rapidly ceases to be perfectly competitive. With unions emerges self-defense for workers, and this tends towards the formation of monopolies and oligopolies. The cost of labor increases. With the increase of wide-spread buying power in developed countries, there is gradually added to elementary biological motivation—work in order to eat—the desire for a certain "necessary extra," even a tendency towards saving and investing, met by today's possibilities of insurance and credit, or by class consciousness. Even though when stretched to its limits "popular capitalism" (in the sense of private stock holding on the part of the salaried class) is probably contradictory and impossible without the collectivization of the means of production and of the product, it still exists in certain proportions: industrial capital disperses, not on the level of manufacturing which continues in the direction of concentration, but on the level of the ownership of shares, bonds, and credits. Small stock-holders, who have little weight in decisions emanating from the boardroom, are unmotivated by the need to direct and organize, by active identification with the firm, or by the pleasure of producing useful goods and services. For reasons of quantity, the investment of their savings, the capitalization of what remains over and above their elementary buying power can in no way be attributed to a will to industrial power; at best these savings represent an increased, delayed consumption, insurance against the risk of helplessness, or protection for family and offspring. To put it briefly, for them motivation is limited to the expectation of a self-increase on the part of their buying power transformed, for a moment, into securities. This is one of the aspects of what is commonly called the dissociation between possession and power. In theory it would not be the same if most shares belonged to the staff of a business, if not the totality of industrial capital to the people.

As for what motivates principal stock-holders, according to whether they exercise their rights directly or are content to delegate them to a salaried, technical directorship, we are either closer to the classic owner-of-the-business or to the modern speculator at the Stock Exchange: the second is moved primarily by profit, and the first possibly only secondarily, in so far as Smith's requirement that profit be maximized remains in force.

On the side of workers who share no ownership in the means of production or of the product, or who own very little of them, factors such as the increase of real wages, the bettering of working conditions, "participation" in the sense of some profit sharing, of understanding the whole picture of the enterprise, information exchange, joint management, even in the sense of some co-ownership of the industrial capital, all these complement somewhat the elementary, biological level of motivation: a taste for extras in consumer goods, for leisure, savings, small investment, interest in premiums for good yield, and in the production of authentic goods and services and of aesthetic and functional values, a sense of the group and various identifications with the enterprise that more or less counterbalance class consciousness. But it still remains that "rank and file motivation resulting from management's positive attitude toward participation," as expressed by Tecoz, encounters some trouble with the fact that it habitually excludes an important participation in profit, which belongs to the private owners of the means of production.[257] [258] Further, experience shows that, under certain conditions and up to a certain point, elementary biological motivation is enough to secure the cooperation of the worker. As for the antirevolutionary role of sufficient participation, opinions are mixed. It is possible, but not certain, that the old adage remains true: "Anoint the peasant king, and he will slay you."

Individual and collective motivations in a collective system.

In a collective system the primary economic motivator can be the common good without necessarily excluding certain profit modalities, even the "optimization" of profit, no more than profit in the preceding system necessarily excludes certain modalities of abundance. Here again the worker initially works because of elementary needs: he who does not work, does not eat. But the rule now applies to everyone, and any surplus belongs to the collectivity that owns the means of production and the product, rewards the individual workingman, and of which along with his family the latter is, in a way, a complete member by right. For this reason, at least in theory, motivation includes a satisfying of justice . . .

To elementary, biological motives, though these be penetrated by a satisfying of justice and an awareness of universal service, can be added other significant motives. Some of these (viewed, to tell the truth, under a different light) are not without analogy to those previously considered with regard to other systems: the level of individual reward, independently of the goods and services distributed collectively, whether it be under the form of salary increase, premiums, or any other form of participation in the product, in business profits; moral and affective participation, the hope of promotion, a work of particular interest, etc. . . The conviction that one is dealing with collective service clearly elicits a certain glorification of labor (overtime, "Communist Saturdays," yield related performances, etc.). But, should the need arise, the collective consciousness is regarded as overriding the enfeebled consciousness of the individual and the right to strike is normally suppressed. How could the owner revolt against himself?[259]

Replacing the old problem of the relations between classes, there arises the problem of the relations between the individual and the collectivity, and that of the latter's structure: there is often a difficult equilibrium between the centralization of the directing consciousness and will (the party's directorate) and centripetal influences (soviets of enterprises and of subsidiary groups); between the living initiative and all levels of bureaucracy from the conception to the execution of the plan; between the organization of production, consumption and exchange, and the actual or possible demand for products; criteria for the division of labor, product, and time . . . Sometimes motivation seems a little weak, or at least inefficacious, and one thinks about the old days when the struggle for life constituted a mighty incentive for unchecked liberalism . . .

Oixos nomia.

Oixos nomia, household administration. If we stick to the freedom and even the obligation to make a profit, and to the administration of collective wealth, the primary definition seems closer to the second. But the freedom and obligation to make a profit can beget certain kinds of abundance, and the overseeing of the common good can be drawn to preserve certain modalities of profit-making as a means.

3 *The Individual Worker's Debt to the Individual,
the Collectivity, or the Group*

In any human or animal society, down to that of parents and offspring, one part of the product of individual labor is set aside as a social levy. This is one aspect of the major biological law of mutual assistance, just as fundamental as the law of struggle and competition.

We have already seen some modalities of social levies, as well as some consequences that these modalities have on the quantity and quality of activities linked to elementary labor or authorized by leisure, on the distribution of labor, product, and time. These warrant some emphasis.

Labor-value, productivity, standardized products, buying power, differential technological profit.

One segment of classical analysis holds that real value (i.e., the selling price) is regulated finally by the "labor-value," or at least it should be.[260] [261] This theory is disputed, and with good reason![262] Some currently noted facts, however, raise the question as to whether it is as out of date as certain economists profess. First, the relative selling price of manufactured goods and services is relatively reduced when they are produced with greater productivity (i.e., with less human labor) and at an optimum rate of production (standardization).[263] Second, there is the differential or marginal profit stemming from the cost differences between methods of production: a technically advanced industry can market each unit at less expense and with greater advantage than the average of other industries. Third, the ordinary man's budget in developed countries has gone through a qualitative change in such a way that the part of his budget reserved for basic necessities has been relatively reduced; the lesser price of standardized products probably has some effect here, along with other factors such as unionization. So we have some reason to wonder whether Ricardo's interpretation does not maintain a substantial validity in many cases of price regulation. This in no way excludes use-value. As for value associated with intentional scarcity and arbitrary valuation, these clearly show up in minimally competitive systems or in systems in which competition has been completely suppressed.

There have been observed at least three profit mechanisms. First, there is cost-free labor surplus resulting from an increase in individual work time without any increase in pay (absolute increase in value). Next there is a cost-free labor surplus that happens as a result of diminution, with no change in the total work time, of the work time necessary for purchasing basic necessities, the value of the latter lessening with the increase in productivity and standardized production (relative increase in value).[264] Finally, there is the "extra" increase in value, i.e., differential technological profit. This last sees its importance grow to the extent that workers' self-defense by the means of unionization reduces the first two. Contrary to what some classical analysts seem to affirm, it does not come from a cost-free labor surplus. It is in inverse proportion to the total quantity of human labor spent on a unitary, concrete quantity of product and in direct proportion to productivity, auto-mation, and the optimization of production output.[265] If currency remains stable, it supports and even implies a drop in the selling price of the product. It appears to involve a triple verification, theoretical and experimantal, nontautological and more elaborated, of Ricardo's theory in a Smithian system when the labor market ceases to be perfectly competitive. We will make no additional mention of price-salary profit margins in a private monopoly or oligopoly, nor of its inflationary significance demonstrated daily by the facts, which possibly constitutes another argument in favor of Ricardo's ideas.[266]

Popular capitalism.
"Popular capitalism," or more exactly stock ownership by the working class in a private capitalist system, has been advocated as a compromise solution between the old forms of private capitalism and the collectivization of the means of production and of the product through revolution or legal means, or it has been rejected as aberrant. In several developed countries an increase in the people's buying power and the dispersion of the ownership of industrial capital is observable. What is the degree of correlation between the two processes? How far can the second go? Given that Ricardo's theory con-tinues to contain some truth (no exchange value for the product and *a fortiori* no profit without work), the question, it seems, concerns what would happen at the limit situation, when each would profit (in the sense employed in economics) from the labor of each, and everyone would work to give profit

to everyone . . . One might suppose at least that a conflict of motives could arise in each, and that the workers' interest in basic labor would decrease in proportion to the increase in the value of securities. A cartoon that appeared in the *Journal de Genève* in 1969 depicted the "new stock-holders" of the Renault corporation, filing into the plant at seven, each dressed in fur-coat and opera-hat, with attaché-case and small dog, to the great astonishment of Georges Séguy and Eugène Descamps!

Value and levies in a collective system.

In a collective, directed, and nationally self-sufficient system, there is an observable tendency towards the authoritarian fixing of production, salaries, and prices, though not necessarily an arbitrary one. There is no unionized defense. It can happen that selling prices are defined by the old notion of labor-value; but once this latter has stopped regulating selling prices as a result of Smith's competition and under the condition of usefulness measured by demand (admitting that it ever truly did), then it must be imposed by authority and would not always correspond to reality, as in the case of nonsellable stocks, the black market, and the impossibility of selling the same product at the same price in both domestic and foreign markets. If we account for a profit when salaries, as a part of costs, and the selling price are fixed by authority, then the same applies to the difference between them, and consequently to the social levy on the individual worker from which an eventual participation in the business product or profit ought to be deducted. The worker on the periphery takes the brunt of the social levy to the extent that a centrifugal direction dominates, and less as participation and mutuality of influence grows stronger. We can surmise that international confrontation between different systems tends to equalize certain rules.

Production, levy, and distribution.

In brief, a social levy on the individual worker's production is a biological necessity. The "marginalist reasoning" cited by Keynes (i.e., the individual worker receives all the product of his labor, but on condition that the output is not proportional and the portion of the product has been calculated for all workers based upon the weakest contribution, that of the most recent contributor) is a joke against nature in its first part, and doubtful in the second. We have seen more authentic forms of marginalist analysis.

If some kind of a social levy is necessary, its modalities are various, and along with these its correlations with the quantitative and qualitative levels of employment and the division of labor, product, and time. Under the form of private ownership of profits, for more than two centuries a large part of the levy has been gotten first by the class that possesses industrial capital; but at the same time this has given impetus to a remarkable economic system, one that is not at all exclusive of technical progress, a certain absolute abundance, and even some sharing. The latter tends towards greater justice, or at least less injustice, to the extent that the system tempers itself in different ways. A second economic system tends to arise from the first. Without necessarily excluding profit as a means, sign and element of accountability, it ceases to regard it as its principal impetus. Perhaps more than towards unrestrained increase in production, consumption, and investment, it is thought to look towards greater justice in the distribution of individual and collective goods; yet on the other hand it appears to involve its own weaknesses too. It seems that in one way or another we manage to avoid the horrendous subdivision of the species that Wells glimpsed for a moment in his *Time Machine*.

Automation and a certain control can certainly contribute to a judicious and more just distribution of the means of human development. As much, however, as freedom or the obligation to make a profit, government that seeks only the common good is in danger of forgetting that a collectivity is not an empty whole, a sum or multiplicity of zeros, a conglomerate of individuals stripped of their own value.

Still other modalities of social levy intervene, such as those related to the size and structure of the population, and contribute to rule our work and our time in accord with our own will or against it.

Geneva
June 18, 1970

Part Five
Appendices

Letter to Monsieur P.

Geneva,
August 7, 1970

Dear Sir:

Once again, thank you for having received me so kindly. I am sorry to have had to beat such a hasty retreat under the pharmacodynamic influence of the Punch cigar!

How can I express my gratitude for having graciously examined the little paper on "economic and cultural problems?" The opinion of one regarded as an expert by the U.N.O., the O.E.C.D., and the G.A.T.T., is precious. My understanding of it is as follows.

You first note that this study does not touch upon concrete, present economic reality in all its detail and complexity; you are sorry that it is not more empirical. It in fact strives to point out some lines of force, internal requirements of systems, conscious or unconscious motivations, relationships between economics and personal development, from an historical point of view as well as from that of our possible hopes and fears, not to say previsions, into the far distant future.

As regards concrete present situations, and particularly those in our own country, it is certain (limiting ourselves to the two examples) that neither Smith's situation of perfect competition nor the situation of strict private monopoly exists in pure state, and probably cannot do so with any durability. You correctly point out that in fact concentration continues to go hand in hand with competition, though it is perhaps true that the latter happens more on an international scale than nationally. A little later you also observe that in fact inflation and technical progress coexist. There is an evident temptation to reconcile these two findings: on the one hand competition would continue to push towards technical progress through the old Smithian necessity to seek after profit by differentiation in technology, i.e., in productivity; on the other hand (in the absence of an authoritarian fixing of prices and salaries and without even asking which leads and which follows, salaries or prices) concentration resulting from oligopolies, trusts or *ententes,* or even simply from a common tendency of producers that lacks the moderating effect of sufficient competition, would favor the "price-salary race," with the producers using every means to maintain or increase the benefit margin including those which do not involve any increase in productivity. Thus the coexistence of concentration and competition would be one means of explaining that of technical progress and inflation. These are probably not the only factors, but such a study is beyond the scope of our project and our competence.

You note that inflation is characterized by an increase in the total amount of money in more rapid turnover than that of the total quantity (how measured?) of concrete goods and services. As to price changes, we are, however, interested in the buying power of people more than in the evolution of the buying power of money. Further, were there need, the growing quantity of free goods and services (clearly on the rise, though more or less rapidly according to systems and countries) would confirm our idea that the real value of concrete goods and services, i.e., their total selling price, and their total quantity evaluated in ways other than exchange-value, can vary inversely.

You call attention to the difficulty of quantifying an "aggregate" of heterogeneous, concrete products other than by price, i.e., according to the coin of the realm: indeed, this is one of the essential functions of money. We have frequently been in very close contact with concrete goods and services, and we are the first to recognize that these pose a problem whenever a quantification at once total and precise must be substituted for a simple category by category enumeration or an extremely global view of things. Initially the general relation does not involve financial considerations: we can add that, in a sense, this relation is more technological than economic. It is framed as follows:

The total quantity of work required of men is in direct rapport with concrete consumption, production, and expansion, and in inverse rapport with automation. The consequences of automation in a limited sector on the quantitative level of employment in the input and output sectors depend on the degree of automation in the latter two (the multiplier of employment.)

As you have noted, this relation is ambivalent in the sense that, according to the conditions of application, it can apply to a diminution as well as an increase in the quantitative level of employment. It is greatly encouraging to see that we are in agreement on the point that, contrary to the opinion of many, automation (or any other way to increase productivity) is not at all contra-indicated in underdeveloped countries with considerable manpower, either underemployed or unemployed, when used selectively. You include the additional precision that the increase in productivity should be focused at the point of "bottle-necks," and you give some concrete examples. Rather than use the terms "input" and "output" previously used by theories calculating on the basis of value, you prefer those of upstream, downstream, confluence, etc. . . .

In several places I have touched on the relationships between the financial point of view and that of the general relation, basically limiting myself to reporting common opinions. Even the idea that, under certain conditions and in a certain fashion, the old Ricardian principle of labor-value continues to be supported by the facts seems to me generally accepted, with whatever level of explicitness. The difficulties certain of us have in admitting it seem to me principally irrational and affective, and are probably due to the fact that the Marxist analysis is in part heir to Ricardo's analysis.

The sale price of a unit of product is a function of its cost price, and the latter continues to depend heavily on the quantity of human labor expended, though this takes place only during the final production cycle. This influence of the quantity of human labor expended on prices is both direct and indirect. It is direct through a reduction of the cost of that production factor, supposing, obviously, that the salaries in a given economy remain at equal levels. It is indirect in the sense that the reduction of the quantity of human labor during the final cycle is in correlation with the increase in fixed capital. When the total quantity of production is sufficiently great (which is brought about technically by the predominance of machines, automation, etc. . .) this fixed capital, even though increased in absolute value, sees its amortization considerably reduced in relation to the concrete unit of product. The term "standardized product" thus involves the double notion of something manufactured at a high level of productivity and in sufficient, let us say optimal, quantity. The lesser price for these standardized products, all else being equal, is one of three arguments *a posteriori* proposed in favor of Ricardo's relevency today. The second is the marginal profit based upon the difference in productivity and in technology between advanced enterprises and the average of other enterprises.

As for the third argument (progressive modification of the structure of popular consumption in developed countries), you correctly call attention to the fact that we can observe changes in the very nature of consumer goods while only the class of use remains the same: thus I have great difficulties in finding pure linen clothing for the warm weather! As for the general difficulty of quantifying aggregates of heterogeneous goods and services other than through the coin of the realm, this is obvious, but we have in view no more than a very approximate insight into one direction of evolution. From this point of view, it seems beyond discussion that, on the whole, the mean of our populations has gone well beyond the chick-pea . . . It does indeed seem that one of the factors involved in this is the relative lowering of prices of goods manufactured at a high level of productivity and in large quantities. But I have only cited Ricardo in passing.[267]

In your opinion the most elementary goods and services will soon be producible in sufficient quantity and able to be distributed equitably; we rejoice in this. But you feel that in relation to these extremely elementary goods and services the substructures (the urban, for example) are literally enormous, and you think as we do that—in respect to foodstuffs or goods of greater sophistication but still somewhat elementary—there remains a very great void to be filled before we must deal, from the planetary point of view, with the problem of exaggerated consumption, production, and expansion and their correlations with our use of time. Further, you make the observation that we are in fact experiencing a progressive, general, and constant reduction in the work week: 35 hours for leading American industries (to which we can add 42 hours for all workers by recent decree in the USSR and 60 hours, according to official figures dating from 1958, for Swiss physicians in socialized medicine,[268] — and this constitutes another reason for rejoicing. We persist, however, in thinking that by pointing out the risks of unchecked, exaggerated, rampant consumption, production, and expansion, we have not, as they say, conjured up a paper tiger.

You still fear, and with good reason, that the growing intensity of work, already noted in classic studies, is off-setting the increase in leisure time by requiring that a large part of it be devoted to recuperating from the fatigue caused by nervous tension.

And, my dear Sir, I am skipping all sorts of other excellent remarks from which we shall derive the greatest profit. I hope that we shall have the occasion to see each other again soon and rediscuss all these matters. Until then, allow me to wish you a good and fruitful vacation.

My wife joins me in assuring you and Madame P. of our best regards.

Some Perspectives on the Dialectical Nature of Progress

In dialectical process, analysis and synthesis, real or at once real and grounded in the real (mental, for example), are linked together and with the dialectical conflict. Real analogy and classification, i.e., a conscious or unconscious reaction to a real analogy, connote composition between identity and difference: they constitute a particular case of analytic and synthetic dialectic. In a sense synthesis may sometimes do without analysis. Plato's dialectic of the sense and the intelligence, reserved to the highest animals and man, cross-checks in different manners the conflicting, analytic and synthetic dialectics. As for N. Bohr's and F. Gonseth's "complementarity," this amounts to a kind of provisional mental synthesis, based on aspects of the real which has been variously modified by some of our analytical procedures.

When two atoms of hydrogen and one atom of oxygen combine through the exchange of two electrons, there results a simultaneous and conjoint act of synthesis and analysis: indeed, the synthesis announces the correspondence between chemical valences. When hydrogen burns in air, oxygen separates from nitrogen and, in a sense, analysis emerges more clearly. Hydrogen is not the only substance capable of being oxydized and oxygen can be taken out of different oxides: the analytico-synthetic processes therefore speak of analogy and act as classifiers. The chemist in turn analyses, synthesizes, and classifies by way of real operations with the test tube, operations that are at once real and grounded in the real within thought. In the course of successive combinations, new properties suddenly arise; those of previously isolated constituents are partly masked. Identical or analogous processes appear at higher and higher levels of organization, to the point where Father Teilhard was able to exclaim: *"it is in love that this obscure intersympathy of the first atoms or the first living creatures is transformed by becoming man."* But this is only one aspect of the question.

In a certain fashion life goes forward through analysis, synthesis, combat, and death. Whether genetic variation does or does not take place through chance alone, the Darwinian struggle for life is a fact as beyond question as mutual aid, and its selective action has clearly been fundamental. The biological necessity for reciprocal adaptation, for an ever greater reciprocal adaptation, spins out its consequences, illuminating Jackson's and Teilhard de Chardin's law of complexity-consciousness as if through a causal nuance. Pavlov's reflexology, ethology, the comparative physiology of behavior show us, with innate or learned reactions to signs, an analogical, analytical, and classifying modality of the relationships. The neurology of the infant, genetic epistemology, and psychoanalysis lead us in their turn to see conflicts, analyses, abstractions, syntheses, analogies, classifications, conscious or unconscious, real or at once real and grounded in the real, their interactions and their role in the increase or progressive manifestation of our ability to understand the whole, to locate the parts in their relationships with each other and with the whole, and to behave accordingly . . . in a word, their role in the progress of consciousness towards the liberty of universality.

For Hegel and several related philosophers, the conflict dialectic sometimes coincides very clearly with the synthetic and analytic dialectic. Sometimes the relationships between these two modalities of dialectic are less clear, or more diversified. The triadic process "thesis-antithesis-synthesis," somewhat theoretical in the eyes of Lenin, and the "negation of the negation" condemned by Stalin in 1938 as offensive, reactionary, and counterrevolutionary, subsequently rehabilitated as a "spiral" modality of progress, do not exclude analysis, conservation, or unification whether these be real or at once real and grounded in the real; quite the contrary. *Aufheben* means to preserve and elevate as well as negate or abolish. "Creative negation" is part destruction, part conservation, and part emergence. The goods of the land and the goods of the sea are first declared exclusive of each other, the part or aspect being erroneously taken for the whole, and then the omission is recognized. Picking blossoms prevents picking fruit, and private ownership of the means of production produces socialism, but here we have only successive moments, standing in a kind of contrast, opposed, not devoid of conservation, perhaps necessary, of processes that are otherwise unitary. Still more profoundly, in the silence is heard the dialogue between self-satisfaction and infinitude, attachment to trifles and the desire for all, incompleteness and a kind of foretaste of a future without limits, a tendency, attraction, or presence . . . God, the Alpha and the Omega, is seen, or believed, to have created man after his image, and man, somehow separated, struggling to be reunited with God. Or the divinized world, for a moment or forever escaping the second principle of thermodynamics, in a momentary or endless process of growth, of organization, as beginning and continuing to achieve self-consciousness in animals, man, in the people, subsidiary groups, the state, the party, in Hegel, through a movement of reciprocal information, not to say of reciprocal creation, a movement that is both harmonius and shaken, from apex to base and from base to apex . . .

Just as much as the existence and nature of the conflict, as its antagonist or nonantagonist character (a distinction recently given greater depths by Mao-Tse-tung), it can be difficult to affirm its interiority or its exteriority, its internalization or its projection outwards, or both at one and the same time. Indeed, if we speak of a difference or of a modification, a contradiction, a contrariety, an opposition, a positivity or a negativity, a presence or an absence, an appearance or a disappearance, a construction or a destruction, a conservation, a composition, a substitution, a sublimation, an emergence, a decomposition, we are first affirming a certain distinction between factors, aspects or moments, the reality of a level of development, the real originality of an individuality in relation, the real unity of a process related to other processes within the whole, to God or within God. The problem of "the unity of contrasts and the struggle between contrasts" is initially that of the realism of mental analysis and synthesis, the very same that distinguish real unities, parts of unities, and conflicts within the "Res Universa."

In his botanical example Hegel successively assumes the perspective of the distinction between moments and that of the vision of the process as a whole, the vision of change. We might well wonder whether synthesis is here doing anything other (already a lot) than declaring that a certain reification of the data of analysis is erroneous. *"Die Knospe verschwindet in dem Hervorbrechen der Blüte und man könnte sagen, dass jene von dieser widerlegt wird . . ."* *"The bud disappears in the blossoming of the flower, and one could say that the bud is refuted by the flower . . ."* We can make an analogous observation about the synthesis of concomitant aspects which initially fail to be recognized as such, i.e., at first are not related back to the unity of an individual or a class. But there are other ways to approach the ancient problem of unity and multiplicity, of permanence and change. I have indicated but some of them.

Theories of Evolution: Some Doubts and Some Suggestions

Schematically, the two principal theories of evolution proposed up until now have been that of "the inheritance of acquired characteristics" (in the sense of transmitting to offspring the individual learning of parents other than by education or by the elimination of potential progenitors with less ability to learn), and that of the selection of chance variations, a selection which provides for the greatest reciprocal adaptation. Neither classical genetics nor molecular biology appear to have added any important modification to these two theories until now.

However, the first of these continues to run up against the lack of certain and systematic observations of the inheriting of learned characteristics (on the scale, it is true, of our own duration). As for the second, given the multitude of amazing mechanisms and behaviors of reciprocal adaptation, both internal and external, observed by botanists, zoologists, ethologists, psychologists, physiologists, physicians, etc., and inferred through analogy or observed by paleontologists, we may well wonder whether observation and calculation have actually proved that the number of mutations presumed to have taken place purely and simply by chance have been sufficiently large to provide some probability for such events happening before they were selected by the necessity of the increase in reciprocal adaptation. It is not so much selection, the conservation of what is more useful and the elimination of what is less useful, as the volume required of chance variations which could create a problem in Darwin's theory. In a word, the marble should contain the statue released from it by the sculptor's chisel and we are not certain that the marble had the dimensions required to contain all that it is thought to have yielded. The engagement of a line of descendants, because of such and such phenotypical behavior relatively independent of the genetic code, within such and such relations, in such and such environmental direction, and consequently in such and such selection pressure, might not be a wholly appropriate argument. Trying all possible anti-bodies, among which the antigen would make its choice only after the fact, no matter how suggestive, perhaps would not constitute a sufficient proof.[270]

The building of functional structures can, it seems, be regulated genetically or extra-genetically by retroactions arising from the phenotype related to its environment. It is not evident that extra-genetic regulation involves no addition of retroactive regulation at the genetic level, higher than the point regulated extra-genetically on the ascending chain. The functioning of a structure may or may not be accompanied by the latter's continued fabrication in whole or in part for the purposes of restoration or growth. Even in the case of possible combinations such as those of a group of supposedly irreplaceable neurones, function goes hand in hand with the myelinization of axons, a prolonged branching out, the production of synaptic substances and enzymes, and, in a general way, a cellular metabolism.

Whether we are dealing with the producing of a structure or the functioning of a structure in some way finalized, the phenotypical explicitation is more or less strictly defined by the genotype, and more or less a function of the environment. We tend to think that "innate" behaviors, those that are quite formed and preadapted, dispensing with learning if not with maturity, exercise, and triggering signs, are circumscribed more strictly by the genotype than are learned behaviors; at the same time, the latter involve more or less durable memory. Finally, ruled at least by their genetic codes and their environments, living beings tend with man towards the liberty of universality, i.e., make progress in the ability to understand the whole, to locate the parts in respect to each other and to the entirety. This ability involves mobility along with conservation and coherence. According to whether we are taken more by the piano or by the melodies, by the print or by the meaning of the text, we will point out one or another aspect to emphasize the possible statistical difficulty in question.

Recall, however, that in numerous cases, particularly in learning behaviors, a virtuality is selected as a result of only a small number of realizations. For example just think of the few realizations that assured victory to our Cro-Magnon ancestors, and of all that the latter (except for later mutations) still contained of genetic virtualities unsuspected at the time that nature made its choice. Natural selection does not judge on the basis of maximal performance, as we do in the case of the prototypes of our automobiles and planes, and even cars and planes themselves evolve. This does not necessarily constitute another difficulty for Darwinism. Paradoxically, we might even wonder whether this may not minimize the difficulty that we are examining at present. Indeed, it seems that the more "simple" have been the early behaviors used to select much vaster genetic virtualities, the greater must have been their probability for a given number of chance mutations.

It is not only the classic Darwinian and neo-Darwinian theories that can admit "chance and necessity" as the sole factors in evolution, genetic mutation happening in a certain way by chance and the need for an increase in reciprocal adaptation joined with differentiation, i.e., the need for unification without confusion between the differentiated organic originalities interrelated within the whole. If serious statistical studies would happen to undermine the supposition that mutations that are purely and simply due to chance have been produced in sufficient number to allow structures and behaviors of adaptation and reciprocal adaptability some probability, a new working hypothesis could perhaps facilitate things. We could suppose that the retroactive influences of the phenotype and the exterior milieu might create an intense functioning within a gene or a group of genes, which would weaken them and increase the rate of mutations at their level. Chance, for chance there will always be, would in a way be focalized by necessity at the requests of the whole, i.e., of the organism in relation, requests that tend toward increase in reciprocal adaptation. The result would be a greater local suppleness with a corresponding increase of the probability in question. The second factor, at least until man exhibits new powers in this field, would be Darwinian selection; the latter would suffice to conserve what is more useful and to eliminate the rest. There is nothing in the first stammerings of molecular genetics that would appear to be fundamentally opposed to this hypothesis. The method of verification—that is, of weakening or strengthening it—would consist in trying to compare the rates of mutations and their qualities among populations that are or are not subjected to particular circumstances of the environment.[271]

Geneva,
August 1, 1973

Bibliography and Notes

1.   F. Engels: Letter to J. Bloch, *in* Ludwig Feuerbach and the End of Classic German Philosophy.

2.   R. Descartes: Discourse on Method.

3.   St. Anselm of Canterbury: Fides quaerens intellectum. Proslogion.

4.   F. Nietzsche: Thus Spake Zarathustra.

5.   H. de Lubac: The Drama of Atheistic Humanism.

6.   R. Garaudy: God is Dead, a Study of Hegel.

7.   G. W. F. Hegel: The Proofs for the Existence of God.

8.   Husserl will take Descartes to task for having escaped too easily from his "egology" after having been trapped in it (maintaining at the same time the idea of an universal mathematics). E. Husserl: Cartesian Meditations. An Introduction to Phenomenology.

9.   E. Kant: Critique of Pure Reason.

10.   V. Lenin: Theory of Knowledge.

11.   The stimulus is only a part of the first term, and its value as a stimulus depends upon the subject. This point will be examined later. It offers no particular difficulty.

12.   J. Hoerni: personal communication.

13.   H. Bergson: Essay on the Immediate Data of Consciousness.

14.   Y. Chesni: *Méthode psychophysiologique appliquée à l'étude du langage.* Cahiers d'Etudes Biologiques, nos. 16-17, Lethielleux, Paris, 1969.

15.   *"Die Knospe verschwindet in dem Hervorbrechen der Blüte, und man könnte sagen, dass jene von dieser widerlegt wird; ebenso wird durch die Frucht die Blüte für ein falsches Dasein der Pflanze erklärt, und als ihre Warheit tritt jene an die Stelle von dieser. Diese Formen unterscheiden sich nicht nur, sondern verdrängen sich auch als unverträglich miteinander. Aber ihre flüssige Natur macht sie zugleich zu Momenten der organischen Einheit, worin sie sich nicht nur widerstreiten, sondern eins so notwendig als das anders ist; und diese gleiche Notwendigkeit macht erst das Leben des Ganzen aus."* G. W. F. Hegel: Preface to the Phenomenology of Spirit.

16.   H. Bergson: Thought and the Mobile.

17.   *". . . intellectus componentis et dividentis, habens fundamentum in re . . ."* St. Thomas Aquinas: On Being and Essence.

18. J. Maritain: Seven Lectures on Being and the First Principle of Speculative Reason.

19. See note 74.

20.   Y. Chesni: *Permanence et changement intérieurs.* Revue Internationale de Criminologie, nos. 1, 2, 3, Genève, 1967.

21.   F. Engels: Dialectic of Nature.

22.   Y. Chesni, F. Martin, H. Schaer: *Sur une malade souffrant d'aphasie amnésique avec augmentation variable de l'intervalle de temps compris entre le début respectivement de la gnosie et de la dénomination verbale; notion de trouble fonctionnel systémique.* Revue de Laryngologie, 87, nos. 3-4, Portmann, Bordeaux, 1966.

23.   So it is that with an infant, in those activities of the brain related to language, a dysfunctional left hemisphere can be replaced by the right.

24.   *". . . corpus requiritur ad actionem intellectus, non sicut organum quo talis actio exerceatur, sed ratione objecti: phantasma . . "* St. Thomas Aquinas, Summa Theologica, Qu. 75, Art. 2, Sol. 3. See also Aristotle: De Anima, and Plato: The Phaedo.

25.   St. Paul: Second Epistle to the Corinthians.

26.   Cf. Bible, Edition Maredsous et Hautecombe, Brepols (Belgique), 1968 (lexique, p. 1604: âme).

27. Cabanis.

28. R. Schaerer: On God, Man and Life according to Plato.

29. Ch. Werner: Greek Philosophy.

30. G. W. F. Hegel: The Proofs for the Existence of God.

31. F. Engels: Ludwig Feuerbach and the End of Classic German Philosophy.

32. H. de Lubac: The Drama of Atheistic Humanism.

33. G. Lukacs: History and Class Consciousness.

34. Y. Chesni: *Méthode psychophysiologique appliquée à l'étude du langage.* Cahiers d'Etudes Biologiques, nos. 16-17, Lethielleux, Paris, 1969. *Inner Words, Dream Thoughts, Phantom Members.* Confinia Neurologica, *31,* 1969; *32,* 1970. *Sur les deux moments cérébraux du langage parlé. Vitesse de parcours des circuits en fonction de l'intensité de la voix.* Revue de Laryngologie, *92,* nos. 9-10. Portmann, Bordeaux, 1971.

35. It appears that what we call "time" is comparisons between changes, regardless of whether or not there is reference to a chronometer (F. Martin, Y. Chesni: *Possibilité ou impossibilité de quelques processus simultanés, ou concomitants avec divers éléments paroxystiques EEG.* Archives suisses de Neurologie, Neurochirurgis et Psychiatrie, *96,* 2, 1965. Y. Chesni: *Quelques remarques sur les rêves dans leurs rapports avec la théorie de la connaissance.* Revue d'Oto-Neuro-Ophtalmologie, *XL,* no. 7, Doin, Paris, 1968. J. Pommez: *Le facteur temps en phoniatrie.* Revue de Laryngologie, *90,* Portmann, Bordeaux, 1969). See Part III.

36. H. Bergson: Essay on the Immediate Data of Consciousness. Thought and the Mobile.

37. A. Lalande: Vocabulaire technique et critique de la philosophie.

38. V. Lenin: Theory of Knowledge.

39. Aristotle felt that the brain was a radiator for cooling purposes.

40. Y. Chesni: *Permanence et changement intérieurs.* Revue Internationale de Criminologie, nos. 1, 2, 3, Genève, 1967.

41.   F. Jacob: The Logic of Living Beings.

42.   F. Engels: The Dialectic of Nature.

43.   A. Lwoff: The Biological Order.

44.   J. Monod: Chance and Necessity.

45.   F. Jacob: The Logic of Living Beings.

46.   André-Thomas, Y. Chesni, S. Saint-Anne Dargassies: The Neurological Examination of the Infant. Spastics Society and Heinemann, London.

47.   Y. Chesni: *Quelques remarques sur les rêves dans leurs rapports avec la théorie de la connnaissance.* Revue d'Oto-Neuro-Ophtalmologie, *XL,* no. 7, Doin, Paris, 1968. *Brèves remarques sur l'abstraction pendant les rêves.* Revue d'Oto-Neuro-Ophtalmologie, *XLI,* no. 7, Doin, Paris, 1969.

48.   J. H. Jackson: Selected Writings.

49.   P. Pavlov: Selected Writings.

50.   P. Teilhard de Chardin: Conférence donnée à l'ambassade de France à Pékin, le 10 mars 1945. Etudes, mai 1946, Paris. Oeuvres, *5,* Seuil, Paris.

51.   K. Lorenz: Essay on Animal and Human Behavior.

52.   Y. Chesni: *Sur le cri et quelques autres comportements mimiques innés examinés pendant les premiers jours de la vie.* Revue de Laryngologie, *91,* nos. 5-6, Portmann, Bordeaux, 1970.

53.   Here again Kant is at once enlightening and specious. Under the name of "categorical imperative" he describes the internal mechanisms, such as noncontradiction in the sense of formal logic, without which logic would cease to be logic, reason would no longer be reason, and man, as an animal with a much greater endowment of reason than other animals, would come to an end. But in so doing he is simply pointing out the contents of a definition. In conformity with his system he saw in this a "fact of reason," a kind of direct grasp of reason by reason itself rather than an "empirically" grounded intellectual knowledge, but this is perhaps of little importance for our concerns. Again, however, the point at which we cease to follow him is when he contends that the exercise of reason as such is not

accompanied by the most profound pleasures (E. Kant: Critique of Practical Reason).

54.   R. de Saussure: *Conduites d'obéissance et conduites d'expérience*. Revue suisse d'Hygiène, *fasc. 5*, 1937.

55.   Mao Tse-tung: On Contradiction. Selected Writings.

56.   Y. Chesni: *Permanence et changement intérieurs*. Revue Internationale de Criminologie, nos. 1, 2, 3, Genève, 1967.

57.   By "environment" we are including organisms of the same or different species along with ecological factors.

58.   Darwin's theory contains two notions: that of reciprocal adaptation, and that of chance variation. The first is common to other theories of evolution.

59.   P. P. Grassé: The Evolution of Living Beings.

60.   A. Freud: The Ego and Defense Mechanisms.

61.   S. Freud: Abridgement of Psychoanalysis.

62.   If by "power," "potency," or "virtuality," is meant that what took place was able to take place, then we are enunciating a truism. If we take it to mean the potency of contraries in the sense of ontology and formal logic, which is to say that what took place might also not have taken place or that other events may even had occured, we will still have to be assured of this. But the theory of the ancients itself tells us that potency can be known only through act. In natural history prediction is frequently no more than an expected repetition based upon several observed repetitions, or an extrapolation. Prediction in applied mathematics—for example in the sense of experimental physics—is without doubt fundamentally the same as in natural history. In the two cases the seeker reasons, that is he actually removes himself for a moment from relationships in a certain way. But in so doing he does not stop pursuing, in a kind of interior shortcut, the very movement of that which he is studying. He proceeds on the basis of premises that have been observed and according to laws of logic common to the whole of the real; for these reasons his predictions will be verifiable.
   To confine ourselves to the living organism, modern biology confirms and makes precise what everyone knows: its development depends at least upon heredity and environment. Some Darwinians and Neodarwinians tend to consider the genotype as

a defined framework, setting out a defined whole of possible phenotypical variations. They do so by basing themselves on two notions: habitual repetition of phenotypical realizations of a given genotype in given circumstances, and variation of these circumstances within certain limits. Nevertheless, without even mentioning the fact that our genotypical text would allow us to understand both ourselves and the universe and to conduct ourselves accordingly, we have no idea whether new circumstances might arise and reveal to us virtualities that were heretofore unsuspected. The problem becomes even more complicated by the fact that we ourselves become responsible for some of these new circumstances. Who could possibly say what might come about given the right time and the right means? Wells had his Doctor Moreau change animals into men . . . And even if he knew something about the possibilities of selection, and about training and drugs, and even if he glimpsed the possibility of grafting machines onto men or fragments of men and *vice-versa*, still Wells imagined nothing about provoked mutations and genetic surgery . . .

Given these considerations and admitting that this word does have a sense, virtuality seems more a property of the whole rather than of the part, or, if you will, of an original reality in relationships. The same thing could be said about setting the limits of an internal contradiction. These problems are linked to those of analysis and synthesis.

63.   See Parts I and II.

64.   Aristotle: Metaphysics, De Anima, etc.

65.   Y. Chesni: *Recherches expérimentales sur la parole intérieure et l'imagination visuelle*. Confina Neurologica, *25*, 1965.

66.   Y. Chesni, F. Martin: *Sur les temps d'évocation visuo-verbale et auditivo-verbo-visuelle comparés à quelques autres temps psycho-physiques, psychophysio-physiques et psychophysiologiques; remarques préliminaires*. Revue de Laryngologie, *85*, nos. 7-8, Portmann, Bordeaux, 1964.

67.   Y. Chesni, P. Dieterle, F. Martin: *Remarques sur les temps de concept et de jugement consécutifs à des stimulations visuelles*. Confinia Neurologica, *25*, 1965.

68.   Y. Chesni, F. Martin, H. Schaer: *Sur une malade souffrant d'aphasie amnésique avec augmentation variable de l'intervalle de temps compris entre le début respectivement de la gnosie et de la dénomination verbale; notion de trouble fonctionnel systémique*. Revue de Laryngologie, *87*, nos. 3-4, Portmann, Bordeaux, 1966.

69.   Y. Chesni: *Méthode psychophysiologique appliquée à l'étude du langage.* Cahiers d'Etudes Biologiques, nos. 16-17, Lethielleux, Paris, 1969.

70.   E. Kant: Critique of Pure Reason.

71.   "Phenomenology" is taken here in the Kantian sense. It would be necessary to make more precise the relations between Descartes' ontological doubt (the *cogito* excepted), Kant's apriorism stripped of existential doubt, and Husserl's phenomenology. It would perhaps appear somewhat artificial and unjust to reduce this last to a simple combination of the worst of Descartes and Kant nuanced by a touch of monadology.

72.   Y. Battistini: Three Presocratics.

73.   In the last Socratic dialogue, "The Phaedo" or "On the Soul," Plato, with particular explicitness, situates the dialectic of the senses and intelligence in a doctrine of the relations between the soul and the body and soul and the Ideas. This follows the "ancient tradition," probably Egyptian and Oriental, and prepares the way for Aristotelian-thomist philosophy. It is one of the great moments in the history of thought.

74.   Along with structural analogies and the definition of structures as systems of selected relations, as theoretical models based on reality, "structuralism" takes its place under the customary rubrics of dialectics. It too sometimes navigates between Charibdis and Scylla, between a closed phenomenology and coincidence. (Cf. Claude Levi-Strauss: Structural Anthropology). Explicitly or not, we have made extensive use of it in this work.

75.   See note 148.

76.   A. Einstein: Relativity.

77.   A. Einstein, L. Infeld: The Evolution of Ideas in Physics.

78.   H. Bergson: Thought and the Mobile. Matter and Memory. Creative Evolution.

79.   G. W. F. Hegel: Preface to the Phenomenology of Spirit.

80.   F. Engels: Ludwig Feuerbach and the End of Classic German Philosophy.

81.   This is the position of Einstein and Infeld, who held that physical theories of the past are not replaced by new ones, but continue to live in them as a particular case within a general case.

82.   R. Tissot: *Notions psychologiques de temps et horloges biologiques*. Symposium Bel-Air III, Georg, Genève; Masson, Paris.

83.   Y. Chesni: *Sur les deux moments cérébraux du langage parlé. Vitesse de parcours des circuits en fonction de l'intensité de la voix*. Revue de Laryngologie, *92*, nos. 9-10, Portmann, Bordeaux, 1971.

84.   Y. Chesni: *Vitesses comparées de la formulation à voix haute et de la parole intérieure chez des sujets normaux et dans quelques cas pathologiques*. Revue de Laryngologie, *79*, no. 12, Portmann, Bordeaux, 1958. *Recherches sur l'activité phonatoire et articulatoire pendant la formulation verbale intérieure*. Revue Neurologique, *102*, no. 6, Paris, 1960. *Recherches psychophysiologiques chez des parkinsonniens avant, pendant et après intervention stéréotaxique sur le noyau ventro-latéral du thalamus*. Archives suisses de Neurologie, Neurochirurgie et Psychiatrie, *94*,2, 1964. *Ralentissement de la parole intérieure et de la parole à voix haute chez deux malades souffrant, l'une de paralysie bulbaire progressive, l'autre de séquelles d'atteinte des deux opercules rolandiques*. Acta Neurologica et Psychiatrica Belgica, *67*, 11, 1967. *Inner Words, Dream Thoughts, Phantom Members*. Confinia Neurologica, *31*, 1969; *32*, 1970.

85.   M. Richelle: *Notions modernes de rythmes biologiques et régulations temporelles acquises*. Symposium Bel-Air III, Georg, Genève: Masson, Paris.

86.   The Rule of St. Benedict.

87.   See Part IV.

88.   Enough sleep, a little stroll, a moment of relaxation, fresh air, a couple of wax plugs in the ears . . . for us these are invaluable aids. In no way do they preclude other pleasures.

89.   Aristotle: Metaphysics.

90.   L. Gallien: Problems and Concepts of Experimental Embryology.

91.   St. Thomas Aquinas: Summa Theologica.

92.   See note 62.

93.   H. G. Wells: The Time Machine.

94.   C. Darwin: The Origin of Species.

95.   It seems that for Jean-Paul Sartre, as for the majority of philosophers and naturalists, a human project would be rational by definition, that is logical and conscious. The existence of a human essence or nature, explicitly denied by existentialism, is therefore implicitly affirmed by it if only in virtue of a simple acknowledgement and a simple criterion of natural history classification. Some other tendencies emerge within the "reasoning animal;" they can be impregnated with biological logic, even though this is not conscious, and they may be found in agreement or in disagreement with themselves and with reason. Can reason choose to dismiss itself? If in one way or another it happened to so do, and if there still existed some zoologists, how might they classify us? What is in question is the meaning and future of reason, of the rational tendency towards universality. The notion of the categorical imperative gives rise to analogous considerations. (Jean-Paul Sartre: Existentialism is a Humanism . . .)

96.   H. Lefebvre: Dialectical Materialism.

97.   "The freedom of the creator, his sovereign capriciousness, can only be exalted at the idea of coinciding with universal necessity. Art is the human prolongation of a cosmic fecundity." (J. Starobinski: Invention of Freedom.)

98.   J. Piaget: Six Lectures on Child Psychology. Biology and Knowledge.

99.   S. Freud: The Interpretation of Dreams.

100.   Y. Chesni, F. Martin, M. Yousfi: *Analyse introspective des rêves et physiologie cérébrale.* Confinia Neurologica, *28,* nos. 3-4, 6, 1966.

101.   Y. Chesni: *Quelques remarques sur les rêves dans leurs rapports avec la théorie de la connaissance.* Revue d'Oto-Neuro-Ophtalmologie, *XL,* no. 7, Doin, Paris, 1968. *Quelques remarques sur l'abstraction pendant les rêves.* Revue d'Oto-Neuro-Ophtalmologie, *XLI,* no. 7, Doin, Paris, 1969.

102.   F. Morel: An Introduction to Neurological Psychiatry.

103.   F. Martin, Y. Chesni: *Possibilité ou impossibilité de quelques processus simultanés ou concomitants avec divers éléments paroxystiques EEG.* Archives suisses de Neurologie, Neurochirurgie et Psychiatrie, *96,* 2, 1965.

104.   W. Penfield, H. Jasper: Epilepsy and the Functional Anatomy of the Human Brain.

105.   W. Penfield, P. Perot: *The Brain's Record of Auditory and Visual Experience*. Brain, *86*, 1963.

106.   H. Feldmann, Y. Chesni: *Troubles paroxystiques de l'audition et de la rémanence auditive*. Revue de Laryngologie, *92*, nos. 3-4, Portmann, Bordeaux, 1971.

107.   Does death amount to our annihilation, to the suppression of all relationship for us, or does it mean a transfiguration? Opinions and beliefs about our ultimate lot are divergent, if not our wishes. Examples are many: the counterparts of the ancient Egyptians; those who died happy deaths and escaped purgatory, to whom one prays and who intercede for us; the continued existence of an intellectual soul separated from the body; the glorious resurrection of the body; and the vision of God face to face if we have loved and sought Him enough here below; the continuation or the end for each of us of a kingdom of God begun on earth; the dissolution of the individual person in the great All; various reincarnations; the immortality of effects, of consequences and of service, after the model of the *Académie Française*.

The Epicurians reassured themselves with the thought that the problem is misstated: we do not encounter death because while we are there is no death, and when there is death we do not exist. For one who is dead, there is no longer any time, and death is nothing. This opinion was later put to words in a song: "*. . . un quart d'heure avant sa mort, il était encore en vie.*" A modern tendency would rather have us pursue long and happy days, lessen our last sufferings and enable us, not too hastily, to experience a peaceful end upon the earth, without any prejudgment about Heaven.

108.   J. Maritain: The Dream of Descartes.

109.   See note 172.

110.   J. de Ajuriguerra: *L'isolation, technique de guérison, règle de vie, voie de perfectionnement*. Symposium Bel-Air II, Georg, Genève; Masson, Paris.

111.   A number of modern biologists emphasize large terrestrial transformations. They maintain that changes in the composition of the air and the sea, in geography and climate, etc., are a cause of massive destruction of species that become inadapted; other species would take their place. It would indeed be a case of "the earth's revolutions," but not in the meaning of successive, global destructions and

creations, or of succesive evolutions *ad nihilum* and *ex nihilo,* the continuity of which would exist only in the divine plan. See: C. Arambourg, L. Cuénot, P. P. Grassé, J. B. S. Haldane, J. Piveteau, G. G. Simpson, E. A. Stensio, P. Teilhard de Chardin, H. V. Valleis, J. Viret, D. M. S. Watson: Paleontology and Transformism.

112.   F. Jacob: The Logic of Living Beings. A. Lwoff: The Biological Order. J. Monod: Chance and Necessity.

113.   That is, at least, the way in which the question of the mechanism of reciprocal adaptation and evolution is translated into the language of molecular biology, including the response, not entirely free of difficulties, which the most classical form of Darwinism gives to it. These problems will be treated more precisely at the end of this book (see Part IV: Theories of evolution: some doubts and some suggestions).

114.   The discovery of the laws governing the transmission of various hereditary characteristics among plants was made by the Augustinian monk Gregor Mendel some years after the publication of "The Origin of Species." H. de Vries called attention to the sudden, discontinuous, and hereditary variation known as a "mutation." Along with Friedrich Miescher, from Switzerland, who initiated the study of the chemical structure of nucleins, Darwin, Mendel, and de Vries stand at the origin of a large part of modern biology. The Russian school, for its part, has for some time shown a tendency towards neolamarckism (Mitchourine, Lyssenko). It has not been alone in doing so: for Paul Wintrebert, for example, *"the somatic modification brought on by the environment would determine the formation within the body-fluids of a kind of antibody which would extend to the hereditary patrimony and be fixed in it under the form of a gene"* (Jean Rostand, Médecine et Hygiène, *XXIII,* no. 674, Genève, 1965, number devoted to the centenary of Gregor Mendel's address to the Society of Natural Sciences of Brünn). Neolamarckism fails to convince Jean Rostand, who at the same time sees the difficulties with the other theory. Must we conclude with him that the mechanism of large organic transformations still completely escapes us? At any rate the need for reciprocal adaptation, and the impossibility that this adaptation could occur other than through a relation, seems to be beyond question.

115.   This is what attracted me to the Pasteur Institute in Paris as a youthful bursar of the Roux Foundation and author of a thesis on the microbiological titration of streptomycine in Monod's synthetic environment. I formed the project of using the reference from the research done on sulfamides in order to compare nutrition in healthy cells and cancerous cells and, in so doing, of being initiated into the study of the elementary mechanisms of life. Circumstances, a lack of interest in botanical

classification, a lively attraction to neurology and psychiatry, and the impossibility of doing everything at once, or even successively, all of these served to direct me partially towards other areas.

116.   J. Monod: Chance and Necessity. Using a particularly simple example, we have here the distinction between the piano and its melodies, between the structural framework, in a way unchanging, and the functional modifications which it supports simply from the point of view of a classifying abstraction, i.e., without any change in title. The first would be more a function of the genetic code, the second more a function of the environment.

117.   Th. Rabinowicz: personal communication. Are these the beginnings, presently ineffective and therefore independent of any selection, of a future race of men with huge brains? Are they only vestigial?

118.   Th. Rabinowicz. *Quantitative Appraisal of the Cerebral Cortex of the Premature Infant of Eight Months*. Regional Development of the Brain in Early Life. A. Minkowski, Blackwell, Oxford & Edinburgh.

119.   J. Leroy Conel: The Postnatal Development of the Human Cerebral Cortex.

120.   Marie Brazier: The Electrical Activitiy of the Nervous System.

121.   J. C. Eccles: *Cerebral Synaptic Mechanisms*. Brain and Conscious Experience, study week September 28th to October 4th, 1964, of the Pontificia Academia Scientiarum, J. C. Eccles, Springer, Berlin, Heidelberg, New York, 1966.

122.   These possible combinations, which are probably limitless in one way and limited in another for a given anatomical structure and genome, would come to progressive realization throughout the course of the evolution of civilizations. Would therefore the natural selection make its choice of neuroanatomical structures by testing only a small part of their functional virtualities? Is this not another difficulty for Darwinism? Would this difficulty be avoided if it were established that some fortunate genetic mutations of the brain took place after prehistory and have been preserved since that time? To this there is added the question of what influence the environment has on individual neuroanatomical development. See note 159.

123.   For partly theoretical reasons, Lorenz insists upon these activities that apparently take place without any object, but the interpretation of such facts demands a great deal of prudence. Indeed how can we be certain that the newborn child who seems to explore with its eyes or suck while sleeping does so without any exterior

stimulation or mental images? The same might be said of the canary or cat, whether awake or asleep, who appears to be grappling with a nonexistent fly or mouse, or of an orgasm that takes place during sleep that is apparently dreamless.

124.   S. Freud: The Destiny of Drives.

125.   K. Lorenz: Essays on Human and Animal Behavior.

126.   Here we have an aspect of what is sometimes called the irreversibility of time: *fugit irreparabile tempus* . . . This does not mean that every change is irreversible; we have just seen this with temporary linkages, a particular case of returning to the initial state. A set of changes is normally more irreversible.

127.   It could be only as a "provisional morality," or as the deliberate choice of a credo, of postulates that are more or less based upon experience and reason but whose degree of credibility is clearly seen, with the will towards internal coherence.

128.   S. Freud: Abridgment of Pychoanalysis. There is a list of Freud's works in the excellent "Vocabulaire de la psychanalyse" by J. Laplanche and J. B. Portales, prefaced by Dr. Lagache.

129.   A. Freud: The Ego and Defense Mechanisms.

130.   R. A. Spitz: The First Year of Life. A Psychoanalytic Study of Normal and Deviant Development of Object Relations.

131.   K. Lorenz: Essays on Animal and Human Behavior.

132.   M. Klein: Envy and Gratitude.

133.   Pierre Termier.

134.   Jean-Jacques Rousseau: Confessions.

135.   Once again we encounter the sameness, resemblances, and differences between the major systems of thought. Some feel that this is explained by an original revelation that was almost immediately obscured by sin: man, as he was just emerging from the state of animality, would have seen God face to face and then in some way would have lost the vision, without, however, forgetting it entirely. It would have been a little like Plato's soul, astray in this world and yet with a vague reminiscence of the Ideas it once contemplated. Others prefer to invoke the com-

monality of objects studied by various systems—reality, man—, the relatively limited number of major explanatory principles grounded in the real and of their mathematically possible combinations. Are the Sun God and Osiris moments in the awakening of consciousness, or its re-awakening? What are the relationships between Ra, Yahweh, and Aton of Amenophis? Is the polytheism of Egypt primitive or secondary? Does it represent more than an enumeration of the names of God? What currents of thought have converged from the far reaches of prehistory to necessitate at one and the same time the survival of the soul, the preserving of the body, their separation and their reunification? (E.g., the rite in which the soul reunites with the corpse through its mouth, and tomb passageways open and oriented towards the sun.) Further information will be found in the excellent book of E. Driotton: Religions of Egypt.

136.   Z. Davidoff: The Book of the Connoisseur in Cigars.

137.   K. Lorenz: Aggression.

138.   F. Nietzche: Thus Spake Zarathustra.

139.   Vercors: Les Armes de la nuit.

140.   Plato: Dialogs.

141.   Aristotle: Nicomachean Ethics.

142.   J. Maritain: The Degrees of Knowledge.

143.   E. Gilson: Introduction to Christian Philosophy.

144.   St. Francis de Sales: Introduction to the Devout Life.

145.   C. Werner: Greek Philosophy.

146.   Lucretius: De natura rerum.

147.   E. Kant: Practical Reason.

148.   "The awakening of consciousness of the whole within the part" is an expression that can lead to confusion. Indeed, for the pantheist or for the atheist, the whole is homogeneous and immanent to itself and each of its parts. For many believers God is transcendent and, in a certain way, apart, and therefore it is better to say:

"proportionate and analogical awakening of the consciousness of God and creation within the creature man." With this precision in mind, we can nevertheless think of the first formula as containing the second, or at least not excluding it, and this would be the case whether or not creation added to God. In all modesty we abandon to the theologians the question of angels, of their existence, spiritual nature, and the conscious activity, superior to that of man, that they would be capable of exercising.

149. Erasmus.

150. Broca.

151. André-Thomas, S. Autgaerden: Psycho-affectivité des premiers mois du nourrisson. Evolution des rapports de la motricité, de la connaissance et de l'affectivité. Masson, Paris, 1959.

152. Y. Chesni: *Sur le cri et quelques autres comportements mimiques innés examinés pendant les premiers jours de la vie.* Revue de Laryngologie, *91*, nos. 5-6, Portmann, Bordeaux, 1970.

153. R. Spitz: The First Year of Life.

154. André-Thomas, S. Saint-Anne Dargassies: Neurological Studies of the Newborn Baby and the Infant.

155. André-Thomas, Y. Chesni, S. Saint-Anne Dargassies: The Neurological Examination of the Infant. Spastics Society & Heinemann, London.

156. Y. Chesni: *La sémiologie nerveuse de l'enfant dans l'oeuvre d'André-Thomas.* Revue Neurologique, *93*, no. 1, 1955, et Livre Jubilaire, Masson, Paris. *Eloge du Docteur André-Thomas,* Archives suisses de Neurologie, Neurochirurgie et Pychiatrie, *95*, no. 1, 1965.

157. J. Piaget: Six Studies in Child Psychology.

158. Concerning Freudian and post-Freudian ideas about oral aggressivity, see note 225.

159. "Genetic limitations" is understood without any general commitment as to unforeseeable effects on individual development arising from unforeseen changes in surroundings and, particularly, from our own action in respect to growth. In the opinion of G. de Morsier, two "mutations" would have occured since the stone age,

characterized by an increase in volume and complexity of the frontal, parietal, and occipital lobes of the brain. The first would have taken place at the beginning of the Neolithic Age, and the second at the time of the Renaissance. An impressive plate shows us the brain of a Papuan placed between that of a gorilla and that of Helmoltz. But what might have happened to this paleolithic man if he had been reared in Geneva? (G. de Morsier: Essay on the Genesis of the Present Scientific Civilization).

160.   F. Martin, Y Chesni: *Possibilité ou impossibilité de quelques processus simultanés, ou concomitants avec divers éléments paroxystiques EEG*. Archives suisses de Neurologie, Neurochirurgie et Psychiatrie, *96*, 2, 1965.

161.   E. Bailleux: *L'option libre et le consentement libérateur*. Revue Thomiste, *LXIV*, no. 1, 1964.

162.   I.e., the confrontation between each of our partial projects and our *Weltanschauung*, our conception of the world and ourselves, our implicit or explicit global project. It is a little like tactics compared to strategy, and the latter to the goals of warfare.

163.   Gabriel Marcel: From Refusal to Invocation.

164.   H. Lefèbvre: Dialectical Materialism.

165.   H. Bergson: Creative Evolution.

166.   E. Kant: Practical Reason.

167.   J. P. Sartre: Existentialism is a Humanism.

168.   A Gide: The Cellar of the Vatican.

169.   "For such is our good pleasure" (some French kings).

170.   "Laisser faire, laisser passer." "Morbleu! laissez-nous faire." (Gournay, announcing economic liberalism.)

171.   Joseph-Arthur de Gobineau: Essay on the Inequality of the Races of Man. See note 159.

172.   For Darwin the submissive, silent adoration of a dog for its all powerful master was the root of religious feeling in man. (C. Darwin: The Descent of Man).

For our part, we would rather have Mrs. Jane van Lawick-Goodall try to understand more deeply the chimpanzee's rites of storm, of thunder, lightening and rain. Does this kind of virile affirmation attuned to the unleashing of natural elements represent a gesture of defense, protection or reassurance? Or is it an expression of aggressiveness, defiance, or joy? Or are we to see in this the beginning of a cosmic communion, of an universal prayer of universality, of a *veni creator spiritus,* or of a twilight of the gods: "O Creative Force, will you, can you penetrate us, pass through us?" And why is it that the females and the children take no part in these rites? (Jan van Lawick-Goodall: In the Shadow of Man).

173.   Y. Chesni: *Sur le cri et quelques autres comportements mimiques innés examinés pendant les premiers jours de la vie.* Revue de Laryngologie, *91,* nos 5-6, Portmann, Bordeaux, 1970.

174.   I. Pavlov: Psychopathology and Psychiatry. Selected Writings.

175.   K. Lorenz: Essays on Animal and Human Behavior.

176.   W. Penfield, P. Perot: *The Brain's Record of Auditory and Visual Experience.* Brain, *86,* 1963.

177.   Y. Chesni: *Petite contribution au centenaire de la théorie de Jackson.* Revue d'Oto-Neuro-Ophtalmologie, *XLII,* no. 7, 1970.

178.   This in no way means that there is a general opposition between the innate or learned "automatisms" and the highest functions of the ego. The latter is built upon many of the former, it makes use of them, and knowingly gives them authority. The reason knows that it is often reasonable not to reason, or to cease reasoning for a moment in order to let them take their own course. (See H. Hartmann: Ego Psychology and the Problem of Adaptation.)

179.   J. H. Jackson: Selected Writings.

180.   W. Penfield, H. Jasper: Epilepsy and the Functional Anatomy of the Human Brain.

181.   Y. Chesni: *Quelques problèmes en rapport avec la névrose obsessionnelle.* Archives suisses de Neurologie, Neurochirurgie et Psychiatrie, *103,* 2, 1969.

182.   S. Freud: Abridgement of Psychoanalysis.

183.   Diagnosis and treatment are practically inseparable. They correspond to the progressive development, often difficult and always filled with unforeseen events, of the conjoint awakening of consciousness for the therapist and the patient, and of the normalization of their relationship.

184.   To reduce what he called the force and the inertia of excitement, Pavlov used bromide. Personally I have had some success with very weak doses of thioridazine, administered over relatively short periods of time such as a few weeks. I feel that diazepan stimulates dreams, or at least their recall. Despite the coincidence that is sometimes observed between the content of a neurotic automatism and that of an epileptic automatism in the case of patients simultaneously suffering from temporal epilepsy and neurosis, I have not made systematic use of antiepileptic drugs such as carbamazepine; indeed, in certain aspects the mechanism of epilepsy seems, despite some similarities, to differ significantly from that of a neurosis. In particular, the cure for neurotics through the awakening of consciousness and the modification of transference does not apply to epileptics. When an epileptogenic center cannot be removed surgically, the latter remain obliged to continue taking medication for an extended period of time, sometimes all their lives. But this does not constitute a sufficient reason to give up trying. The combination of analytical psychotherapy and pharmacology looking to a radical cure for neuroses is an area that is still largely unexplored.

185.   The impact of adequate mental hygiene in the area of neuroses, from the perspective of society in general and criminology in particular, is not always understood as it should be. Not only is the patient suffering from a neurosis ill-adapted, in pain, and unhappy, but his illness normally has very unfortunate social repercussions. The spouse, children, relatives, and group suffer in their turn. Neuroses constitute one of the major causes of conjugal misunderstandings and divorce, so harmful for children, at least under our present structures. There is certainly a considerable proportion of felonious acts directly or indirectly related to neuroses. There is oral dependence, to which some psychiatrists assign an important role in toxicomanies, along with the *"malaise de la civilisation"* and distribution *largo manu* of various tranquilizers and euphorics, a bad precedent and the first step towards drug abuse (and very probably a cause of numerous traffic accidents). There are exacerbated infantile aggressiveness, poorly integrated and sublimated, and hatred between child and parent or child and child, unconsciously transferred in other situations. There are sexual perversions, and in particular that union between aggressiveness and sexuality, innate in certain species of animals and subject to learning in others, that leads to sadism. There are the absurd identifications with the other sex, with "supermen," and with all manner of gangsters when authentic models are missing. There are other harmful consequences of failures in social adaptation.

Even in the realm of more or less long term economics, the true interest of the collectivity, of society and its different subsidiary groups, demands a well thought out approach to mental hygiene. There are economies that are morally and financially prohibitive. Prophylaxis and early treatment of neuroses should be accentuated. These are indistinguishable from the treatment of neurotic adults, who are, to tell the truth, no more than overgrown children in an adult world. One misunderstanding ought to be avoided: it is not true that material aids are contraindicated in analytical psychotherapy. Certainly we feel that the patient ought to make a personal effort, but one that is obviously proportionate with his financial means. In one of his last articles, our master, Dr. Raymond de Saussure, President of the European Psychoanalytical Federation, again made mention of this. In our opinion, this ought to be one of the objects of Social Security in developed countries.

Punishment itself in the juridical sense, while retaining its triple value as a protection for others, as intimidation, and as example, is taking on an increasingly educative role, and even a psychotherapeutic one. This is an encouraging tendency, yet with full realization that it involves the risk of deviations and excess. (Y. Chesni: *Diagnostic, traitement et prophylaxie des névroses. Intérêt en criminologie*. Revue Internationale de Criminologie, no. 3, 1972.

186.   D. Adler, M. Menthonnex, C. Rivier: *L'intégration professionnelle et sociale des élèves de classes spéciales*. Pro Infirmis, no. 1, 1957.

187.   Y. Chesni, M. Fert, C. Balavoine, A. Menthonnex, R. Guyot, S. Dupuis, E. Amblet, A. Paunier, F. Guignard, F. Martin, A. Grillet: *Travaux du Service Médico-pédagogique de Genève*, introduction par F. Naville. Médecine et Hygiène, Genève, 1957.

188.   Y. Chesni: *Retard de langage chez l'enfant. Recherches statistiques sur la dyslexie spécifique*. Revue Neurologique, *101*, no. 4, 1959. *Le Service orthophonique des écoles et les classses de lecture*. Médecine et Hygiène, no. 384, 1957.

189.   Y. Chesni, A. Menthonnex: *La place du travailleur social dans l'équipe médico-pédagogique*. Cahiers Médico-sociaux, no. 1, 1957. Médecine et Hygiène, Genève.

190.   Sully.

191.   The program of the Twenty-second Congress of the Communist Party of the U.S.S.R. proposes the age of two hundred as the first step (The Principles of Marxist-Leninism, Second Edition, Foreign Language Editions, Moscow).

192.   Saint Paul: Epistle to the Corinthians, *I*, 13.

193.   K. Lorenz: Aggression.

194.   N. Tinbergen: The Social Life of Animals. The Study of Instinct.

195.   J. H. Fabre: Entomological Recollections.

196.   It is said that in certain Latin American countries there may have existed institutions devoted to the perfecting of torture.

197.   See note 148.

198.   H. Bergson: The Two Sources of Morality and Religion.

199.   See note 172.

200.   K. Lorenz: Essays on Animal and Human Behavior.

201.   N. Tinbergen: The Social Life of Animals.

202.   K. von Frisch: The Life of Bees.

203.   J. Huxley: The Ways of Instinct. Ants and Termites.

204.   There is not the slightest trace of antimilitarism in this remark: as long as there are aggressors it will be necessary to have soldiers, and a soldier is forbidden to discuss or make decisions in his leader's place. But it is dangerous in its restrictiveness to reduce civil virtues to military virtues, and, in the domain of the military itself, the trial at Nuremberg has judged that there are limits to the delegation of reason.

205. Kéba M'baye, P. Ricoeur. R. Aron, I. Sachs, H. Marcuse, J. Daniélou: La liberté et l'ordre social. Rencontres Internationales de Genève, 1969, La Baconnière, Neuchâtel. We are dealing with an ideal, an orientation, and a counsel.

206.   Mohammed Aziz Lahbabi: Le personnalisme musulman.

207.   "Gifts" is here taken in the genetic sense. According to Darwinian theory the diversity of individual genetic endowments would be the matter for evolution, for progress and for life. Whatever, with man evolution becomes human, and neither

genocide, nor mass sterilizations, nor the breeding of tall, dolichocephalic fair-haired men and women or other human types constitute human solutions. This does not mean that we have to systematically encourage the less endowed to procreate and to discourage those more endowed. From the strictly Darwinian point of view, if we admit that monks and priests have always been recruited from those more gifted in certain respects and according to certain criteria, then the Catholic Church, as Voltaire once observed, would have been practicing reverse selection for twenty centuries!

208.   It seems to us that in this perspective we should examine that other remark of Mao Tse-tung: *"in a class society nothing exists of human nature that is not clothed with class characterization."* The same could be said of sex, race, individuals, etc. We are dealing with a problem much more practical than a discussion about analogical abstraction or the degree of reality possessed by the universals.

209.   China, the Way of Socialism, texts from the Geneva exposition, March, 1972. Ed. Peuple et Culture, Genève.

210.   The sufferings of the peasants under the old regime in China have been depicted in a kind of crèche scene or stations of the cross somewhat resembling our *"santons"* of Provence.

211.   See Lenin: Imperialism, The Final Stage of Capitalism.

212.   See Part IV.

213.   C. Darwin: The Origin of Species.

214.   C. Darwin: The Descent of Man.

215.   K. Lorenz: Aggression.

216.   H. Hartman: Ego Psychology and the Problem of Adaptation.

217.   Added to innate behaviors, the fear of punishment, the attraction of rewards, the introjections of the super-ego, the rationality of the ego, our tendency towards universality, the immensity of our desire, and even, according to some among us, the supernatural movements of grace—there is perhaps still another source of morality and religion in certain early relational habits, more or less overlaping formal group injunctions, which, by their tenacity and their tendency towards analogical transference, can help motivate or at least nuance our broad life attitudes. Is it necessary to

recall the pious childishness of St. Theresa of the Child Jesus: *"I am an exhausted little child," "let the good Papa God do, he knows well what his tiny baby needs"?* (Dom Marc-François Lacan, Bulletin de l'Abbaye d'Hautecombe, 83, juillet-septembre 1971.) Is it necessary to recall the passive obedience to the elder males of the herd, to princes, to *"Führers," "petits pères des peuples,"* all manner of hierarchs, to priests, to strictly codified divine prescriptions? Systematic, un-reasoned contestation and opposition? The ritual murder of the Father? The astonish-ing cry of liberation: "God is dead," as if one could be limited by the All? The identification with Christ? The *veni creator spiritus?* And what are we to say of such expressions as "our mother country," or "our holy mother Church?" . . . of attach-ment to the Blessed Virgin, Mrs. Gandhi, Mrs. Golda Meir, or the Queen of England? . . . Of passive or active identification with the industrial enterprise? There are other societies in which people prefer to be called brothers, with all the love and hate, fighting and assistance, found among true brothers . . .

218.   These are, in a sense, associations for human development.

219.   Emile Male: French Religious Art in the 13th Century.

220.   E. Bailleux: *L'option libre et le consentement libérateur.* Revue Thomiste, *LXIV,* no. 1, 1964.

221.   R. Descartes: Discourse on Method.

222.   *"Such extremes of happiness [. . .] than which I believed life could offer nothing sweeter nor more innocent."* (R. Descartes: Discourse on Method.)

223.   St. Benedict: Rule, First Chapter, *Kinds of Monks.*

224.   Manifesto of the Communist Party.

225.   We are well convinced that "love" is a somewhat devaluated word. Neverthe-less, behind all the diversity of notions and a lot of hypocrisy and unconsciousness, it signifies our interest in being and in beings, our instinct towards relationship, in sum, our realism; but in that sense it does not exclude combat. For Father Teilhard, human love is the blossoming of an energy of attraction, convergence, synthesis, and emergence which assures (or helps to assure), step by step, the dialectical progress of the real towards ever increasing complexity and consciousness: *"it is in love that this obscure intersympathy among primeval atoms or living beings becomes transformed and humanized."* . . . Love, in a way, would be measured by the increase in the quantity of information, of negative entropy. Nevertheless, in material as well as in

spiritual progress, synthesis, composition and integration can require analysis, decomposition, disintegration, and a process of sorting out. Just as much as conservation, the destruction of the old can be the condition of the building up of the new and the suppression of the less good, the condition of the emergence of what is better. Life can have need of death, being of annihilation. Freud, for his part, developed by Abraham and by Melanie Klein, after having opposed autoconservation to sexuality, ended up by setting against each other "the instinct for life" and "the instinct for death," Eros and the pleasure in aggression and destruction and the fear of death. In point of fact, among a number of animals including man, sucking at the mother's breast follows the parasitism of the placenta and prepares for the hunt, the consuming, digestion and assimilation of prey, along with other kinds of social relations, and confusions may result . . . Later, in our slaughter-houses, we set about to nourish others as well as ourselves without anger, if not without aggression. While waiting for synthetic pills, even vegetarians have submitted to the law of mutual devouring among living creatures. "Libidinal drives" and "destructive drives" come into conflict, support each other, mix with each other, are displaced or sublimated, as they connote, produce or help produce the development of individuals and societies and the evolution of species.

226.   A. Smith: The Wealth of Nations.

227.   The maximizing of profit appears to be coessential to the system. Even if Smith's entrepreneur has other motives for entering the system and remaining within it, as long as he takes part in it he is subject to that internal necessity proper to it: the enterprise that is the most profitable has the best chance of survival.

228.   See note 263.

229.   K. Marx: Das Kapital.

230.   The maximizing of profits would be less necessary in a private oligopoly than in a free enterprise system as imagined by Smith. See note 258.

231.   For J. K. Galbraith, regarding the remnants of competition within a private oligopoly, it would not be "good form" for a large firm to try to compete with another by lowering its prices.

232.   In the theory of inflation "by exaggerated revenues," the benefits would bring about an accentuation in the demand for investment and consumer goods, thus provoking the rise in prices. Salaries would lag behind. Renters would face ruin. Some governments claim that they are obliged to accept a certain amount of inflation

in order to maintain a certain growth of the gross national product and avoid unemployment (cf. Richard Meuli: Principles of Political Economy). Still more simply, we can speculate whether profit might not correspond to an increase in the quantity of money exceeding that of concrete goods and services, and whether this might not be an additional argument in favor of a certain currency of labor-value (see note 254 and Samuelson, 262).

233.   Edward S. Mason: Economic Planning in Underdeveloped Areas. The beginnings of the rise of Japanese industry were planned by the imperial government.

234.   J. Rose: Automation. Its Uses and Consequences.

235.   Concerning the relationship between growth and profit and on the corresponding motives in large modern industries, see note 258.

236.   China, the Way of Socialism, exposition of March, 1972, Geneva.

237.   Ota Sik: The Truth about the Czech Economy.

238.   In the U.S.S.R. the work week is presently 41 hours, the retirement age for men is 60, and for women 55.

239.   Other factors intervene in lowering the price of standardized products. See note 263.

240.   The concentration of capital is considered here from the perspective of the business, not from that of its owners.

241.   V. Lenin: Imperialism, the Final Stage of Capitalism.

242.   R. Lattes: Mille milliards de dollars.

243.   See note 258.

244.   See note 232.

245.   I.e., "growth for the sake of growth," or growth and profit taken together. See note 258.

246.   Ota Sik: The Truth about the Czech Economy.

247.   The collective ownership of the means of production and of the product would not necessarily exclude a certain automony for business enterprises, a certain competition, and certain positive consequences of the latter observed in a free system. The difficulty would be the artificial character of the struggle for life.

248.   For J. Galbraith, the large private oligopolies would be practically untouchable. Antitrust legislation, which in a way is antinatural, would apply only to small and medium sized businesses.

249.   The oscillation betwen the predominance of centralization and that of decentralization, even of disintegration, is a commonplace of history. It is not always at the economic or strictly economic level. The evolution of ancient Egypt is one of the most outstanding examples of this. Today the capabilities of communication, the media and computers, have, so to speak, shrunk the planet. These obviously facilitate certain modalities of centralization and centrifugal influences, but they can just as well favor decentralization and centripetal influences. The two processes are perhaps not exclusive of each other. The one and the other are observable in the living organism.

250.   See note 263.

251.   Concrete is taken in the sense of fully real, which does not exclude quantification in terms of the monetary system but is not reducible to it. One and the same quantity, measured more concretely, of the same product can change in value independently of the value of money. It is not inexact to introduce the notion of expansion into the general technological relation, but it is also possible to consider that we are dealing with a redundancy, a pleonasm, since expansion is defined as the increase in concrete production and in the means of production. The validity of the general technological relation is not limited to the case of exponential growth in production, current consumption, and creation of industrial capital. Finally, it is clear that the amount of the concrete product reserved for repairing and increasing industrial goods, i.e., for upkeep and investment purposes, can contribute towards maintaining and increasing automation and thus serve to reduce human labor, but only for the next production cycle.

252.   J. M. Keynes: The General Theory of Employment, Interest, and Money. See also note 232 (the theory of inflation; increase in demand through the increase in revenues, etc.).

253.   A. Huxley: Brave New World.

254.   The classical analysis is here directed toward the theoretical case of the businessman-owner in a context of perfect competition. As for the small stock-holder, he is interested only in the revenue and the increase in value of his shares. Their market price depends, among other things, on the actual or presumed quantity and distribution of dividends and self-reinvestment. The management of modern businesses more or less takes this new factor into account (see note 258). Further, modern enterprise manifests a propensity to borrow and, to the extent possible, repay in devalued money. Here, it seems, is an aspect of inflation born in America during recent times; worldwide American industrial debts would be repaid by increasing output at the Mint (see note 232). One way to slow the process is to restrict credit, and to limit the influx or use of foreign assets . . . almost to the point of imposing negative interest.

255.   K. Marx: Das Kapital.

256.   C. Dickens: A Christmas Carol.

257.   H. F. Tecoz: *Le management*. Impact, mars 1970, Hugo Buchser, Genève.

258.   John Kenneth Galbraith affirms that, in large enterprises, large share-holders (concentrated capital) have lost just as much decision-making power as have small share-holders (dispersed capital). They either lack sufficient shares to control the business, or they possess a sufficient amount of them but, as in the case of Billy Rose and American Telephone and Telegraph, they lack the required psychological disposition and competence. Having no ability to become interested in other things, capitalists of every caliber would be interested in money alone. For Galbraith this seems to mean that their primitive source of motivation is the "maximization" of profit, whatever risks this might involve.

But they would even be powerless to impose this objective on the "tech-nostructure," i.e., on the technical managers. These latter, indeed, because of their high degree of specialization, would be excessively rare in the labor market. It would not be enough to pay them well: they would be literally irreplaceable (as experienced recently by the principal owners of two large American car-makers).

These new managers would be content with large salaries and identification with the enterprise, an identification that would increase with rank. They would not abuse their power in appropriating the means of production and product. Their only interest would truly be growth for growth's sake. More prudent than the stock-holders, they would be wary of the maximization of profit because of the risks involved. Further, by virtue of a notable diminution in competition between large firms, against which antitrust laws would have lost all practical application (a body of law just as unnatural for Galbraith, it seems, as for Marx and Lenin), the maximization of profits would cease to be a necessity inherent to the system.

It is true that the proportion and distribution, the motives, the characteristics of profit interests, the power, and, generally speaking, the importance of industrial share-holders, large or small , concentrated or dispersed, vary according to the kind of business. It is hard to deny, however, that a certain optimization of profits continues to be in correlation with the maintenance and growth of the business, the struggle against what remains of competition, the distribution of sufficient dividends, the self-financed reinvestments, etc. In sum, the technical managers would make the owners of capital stop acting as if they were exuberant participants in some mindless game, ready to run the greatest risks in order to win more; they would be made content, in a word, with profits which are perhaps smaller for the present, but which lead to long term, more secure advantages, with "family investments." But is this distinction between the maximization and the optimization of profits anything more than a game of words?

Not only would the technical managers be the new masters—the obverse of what remains of the "proletariat," even of Marx's "servants of capital,"—not only would growth be their sole objective, and even a growth correlative with optimum profits alone, but in addition the combined needs of growth and private planning would require an overturning of market relationships. Henceforth, the consumer, suitably trained (and, according to Keynes' great principle, sufficiently rewarded) would consume ever more no matter what, to the point of oil blackened seas, polluted water, industrial wastes, smog, noise, to say nothing of other goods that eat away at man's time and his development.

Nevertheless, Galbraith anticipates that there will come a day when these ultraspecialized, cultureless technicians will see the light, cease to believe in growth for growth's sake, and, instead of therefore proceeding to collective appropriation, will restore industry to its authentic function. This latter consists in assisting us, not hindering us, in our growth as human beings, and furnishing us without any kind of over-burdening, without stifling us spiritually, in an equitable distribution, and in reasonable quantity and quality, all the material goods that we need.

In this work Galbraith pays scant attention to the fact that two thirds of the people on this planet are still underfed. It is not his purpose to examine the contradictions of "popular capitalism" in the sense occasionally intended. He speaks hardly at all of the outermost circle, the most neglected of the large industrial firms with a predominance of American capital: foreign labor . . . (J. K. Galbraith: The New Industrial State).

259.   M. Laptine: Leninist Principles of Stimulus to Work.

260.   D. Ricardo: Principles of Political Economy and Taxes.

261.   K. Marx: *Critique of Political Economy. Das Kapital. Wage, Price, and Profit. History of Economic Doctrines*, etc.

262.   P. A. Samuelson: *Economics. An Introductory Analysis.*

263.   According to how it is used, automation can correspond to an increase, a stabilization, or a diminution in the total quantity of production or of the flow of production in comparison with the so-called extensive production accompanied by weak productivity. All else being equal, reducing the production cost of a quantitative unit of product manufactured with greater productivity and a higher degree of automation clearly implies an *optimum* situation in total production and the flow of production, calculated in function of the amortization of capital invested in machinery (standardized products).

264.   K. Marx: *Das Kapital.*

265.   See note 263.

266.   See note 232.

267.   There is perhaps an additional argument in the relationship between inflation and profit (see note 232).

268.   Through the medium of conventions, physicians are little by little ceasing to belong to a "liberal" profession and are becoming, directly or indirectly, salaried employees. The parties of the left as well as the right rejoice to see the ranks of the salaried class thus increased. Industrial principles are increasingly applied to medicine. I am thinking chiefly of the parceling out of work, not in the sense of a specialization that crowns a basic scientific and medical formation, but in that of the breaking up into almost paramedical professions, which require less and less formation time and so reduce the cost of that factor of production. Even though employer associations continue to place physicians on their subscription lists, the class consciousness of the latter is tending to change in turn. Economic analysis has observed and foreseen such transformations since the last century.

269.   Communication to the annual meeting of the Société romande de Philosophie, Rolle, May 27, 1973, concerning the discussion of Georges P. Cottier, O. P., on the Thomistic doctrine of oppositions as related to Hegel's dialectic.

270.   J. Monod: Chance and Necessity.

271.   See also Darwin: The Origin of Species (concerning some laws of variations), and P. P. Grassé: Evolution of Living Beings (including a criticism of Darwinism).

136B064